the interior designer's

bedspread and canopy sketchfile

the interior designer's

bedspread and canopy sketchfile

edited by
Marjorie Borradaile Helsel, ASID

WHITNEY LIBRARY OF DESIGN
an imprint of
WATSON-GUPTILL PUBLICATIONS/NEW YORK

Manufactured in the U.S.A.

Library of Congress Cataloging in Publication Data
Helsel, Marjorie Borradaile.
    The interior designer's bedspread and canopy sketch-
file.
    Includes index.
    1. Coverlets. I. Title.
TT403.H44   746.9   74–26755
ISBN 0–8230–7290–8

First Printing, 1975

contents

preface

The Interior Designer's Bedspread and Canopy Sketchfile begins at the precise point where ready-made, store-bought bedspreads end. Its realm is the world of the custom-made—a world born on the interior designer's drawing board and developed in the professional workroom.

Like the preceding *Drapery Sketchfile,* I have assembled this collection of drawings with a triple intent:

First, it is a design tool. The sketches may be used to supplement workroom orders and instruct workroom personnel. This book sums up and draws together in a single reference the diverse personalities of the bed, with all its multifarious trappings.

Second, it is a catalog in an area where cataloging is presumably unfeasible: How do you catalog what is not available? However, *The Bedspread and Canopy Sketchfile* does catalog a representative amount of the custom-made potential within the specific topic. With it, the professional designer can "show" a client a substantial selection of solutions for the bed without drawing dozens of preliminary designs.

Third, it is an idea source, intended to generate fresh creations and trigger ingenious solutions to old problems.

Although the subject matter seems to be endless, I have surveyed and established its logical subdivisions, even if only briefly in some cases. For instance, the designs in the **quilting and appliqués** category merely hint at the possibilities that exist beyond familiar and standard quilting patterns. A great deal more space is allotted to canopies and bedspreads in three subdivisions: **period, formal,** and **casual designs.** Period designs dovetail with the traditional breakdown of furniture styles and are followed by formal and casual solutions, respectively. Canopied beds with suitable bedspreads lead off each section and then bedspreads alone follow.

For uniformity, **headboards and daybeds** are sketched in studio or twin-bed size in most instances, but the designs can be adapted or expanded quite easily to full, queen, or king sizes. Although it's unusual to find headboards and daybeds indexed together, the distinction between the two is seldom more than the number of ends. Hence, designs suitable for one are invariably suitable for the other.

The category of **skirts** necessarily overlaps with other designs because there are coordinated skirts with all the coverlet spreads. But some skirts cannot be included in the bedspread sections and need separate representation.

The very nature of bedspreads and canopies allows many opportunities for appliqués and trimmings. A myriad of braids, ruffles, and bows is already available or can be executed in a good workroom. Therefore, here, as in the earlier *Drapery Sketchfile,* very little explanation about them is necessary—you'll know best how to achieve the results you want. I have annotated the drawings only where it's desirable to supplement the meaning of the sketch or suggest a certain material.

There are 238 drawings in this volume, assigned to the six categories previously mentioned, with some unavoidable overlap. If you want inspiration on bedspread designs, try thumbing through the canopy sections for solutions that are not repeated elsewhere.

Marjorie Borradaile Helsel, ASID

period
designs

Renaissance

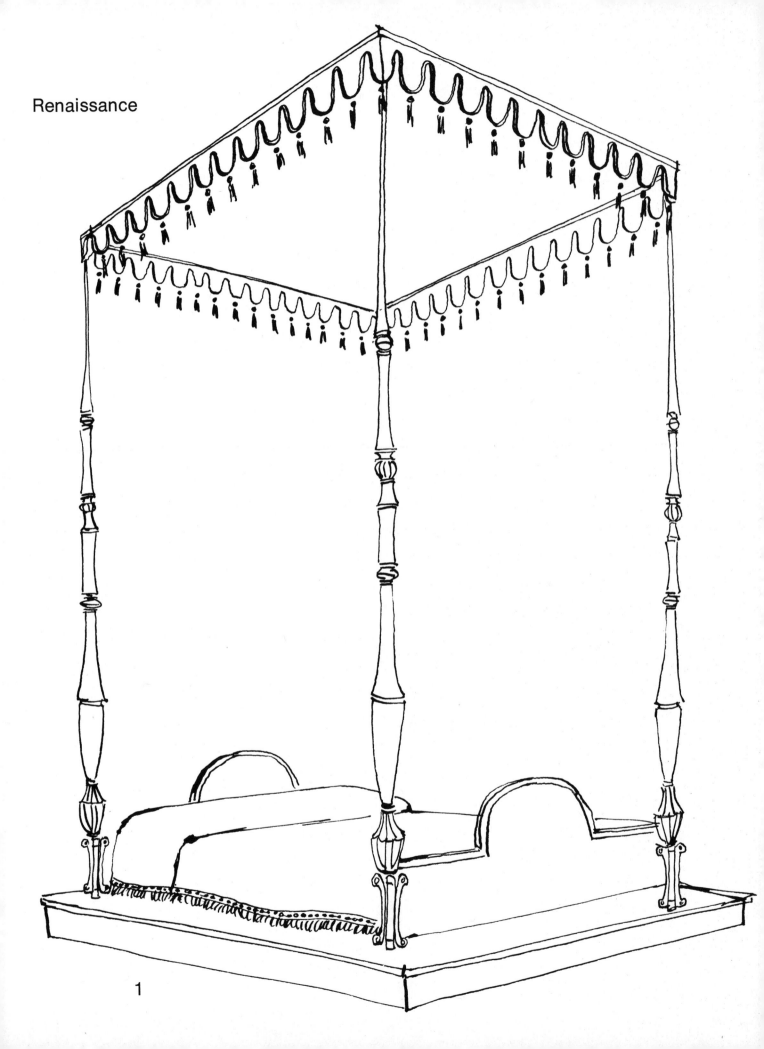

1

Renaissance

2

Renaissance

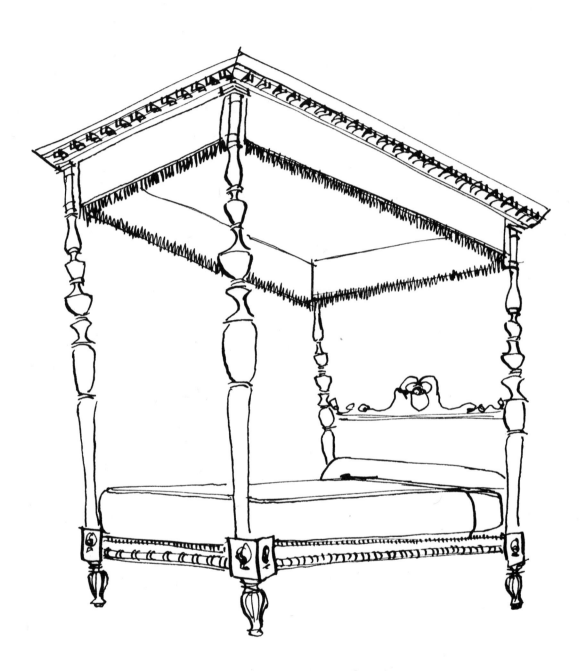

Renaissance

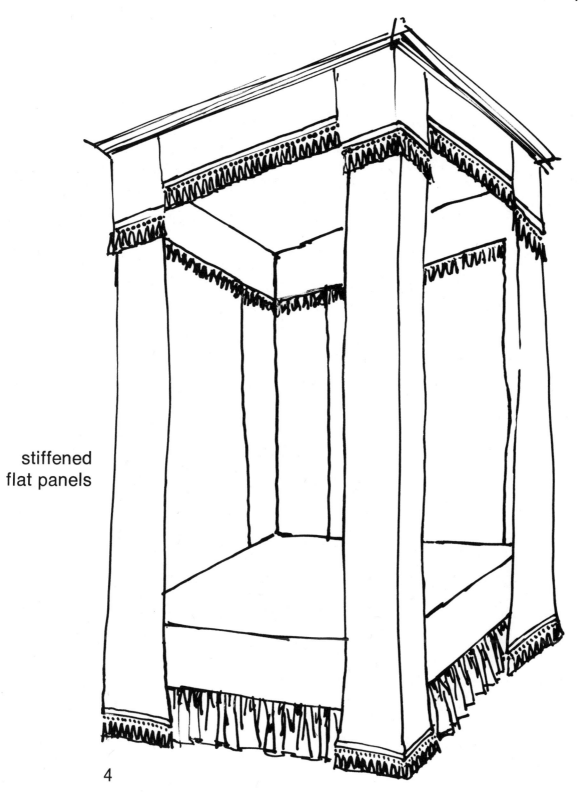

stiffened
flat panels

4

5

Louis XIV

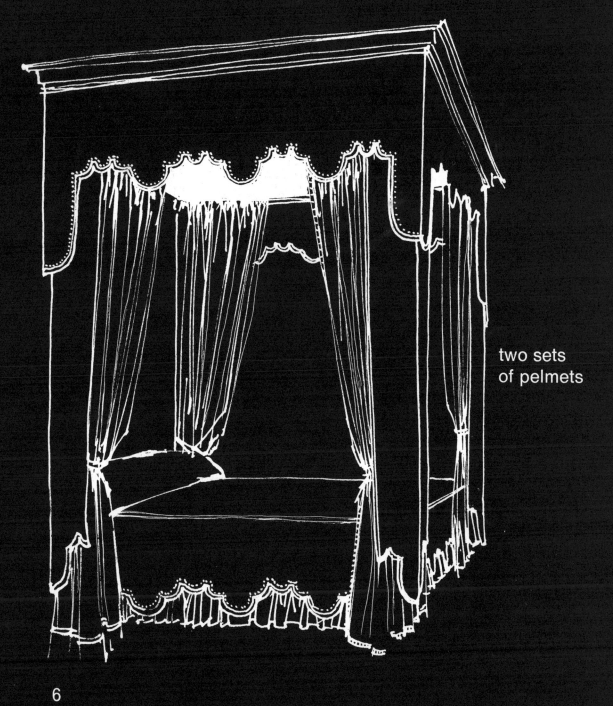

two sets
of pelmets

6

Louis XV

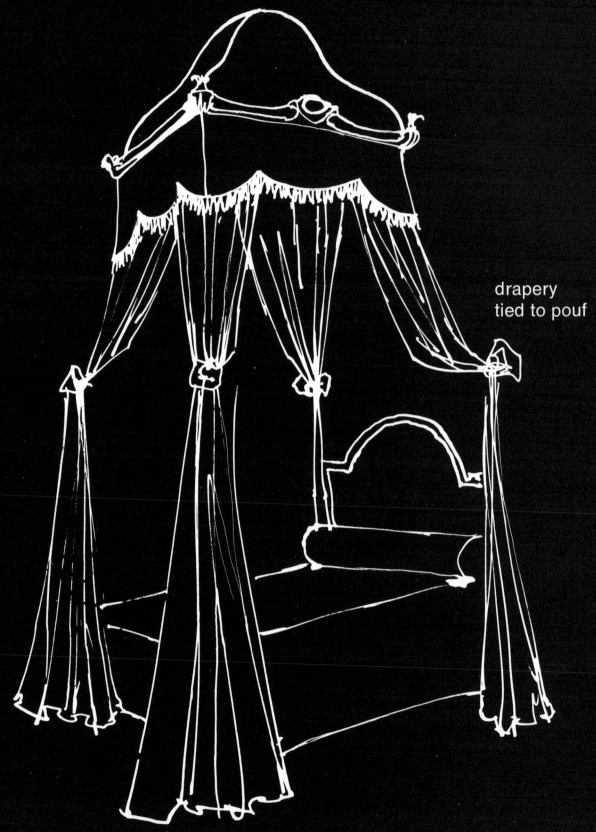

drapery
tied to pouf

7

Louis XV

8

Louis XV

fabric pouf

9

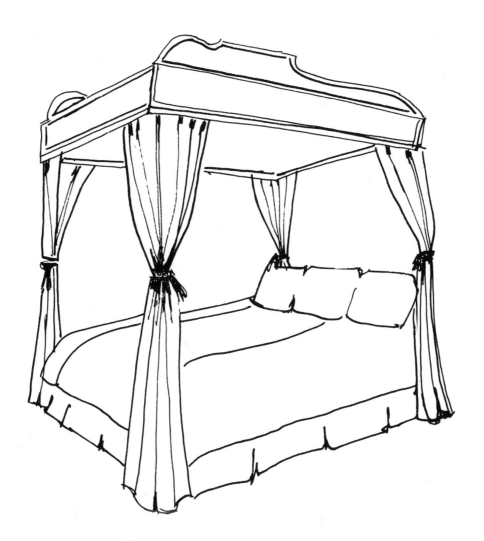

Louis XV

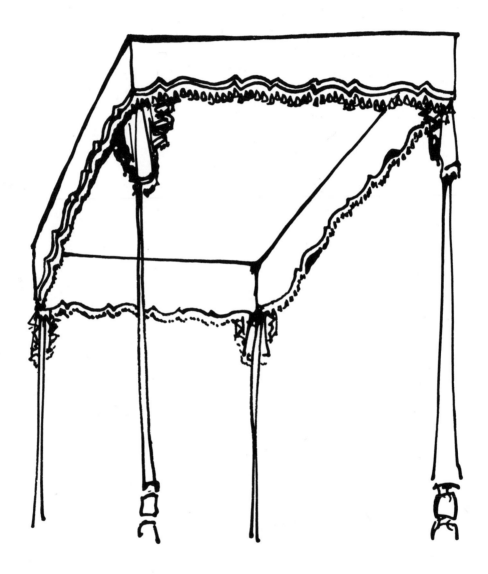

11

Louis XV

12

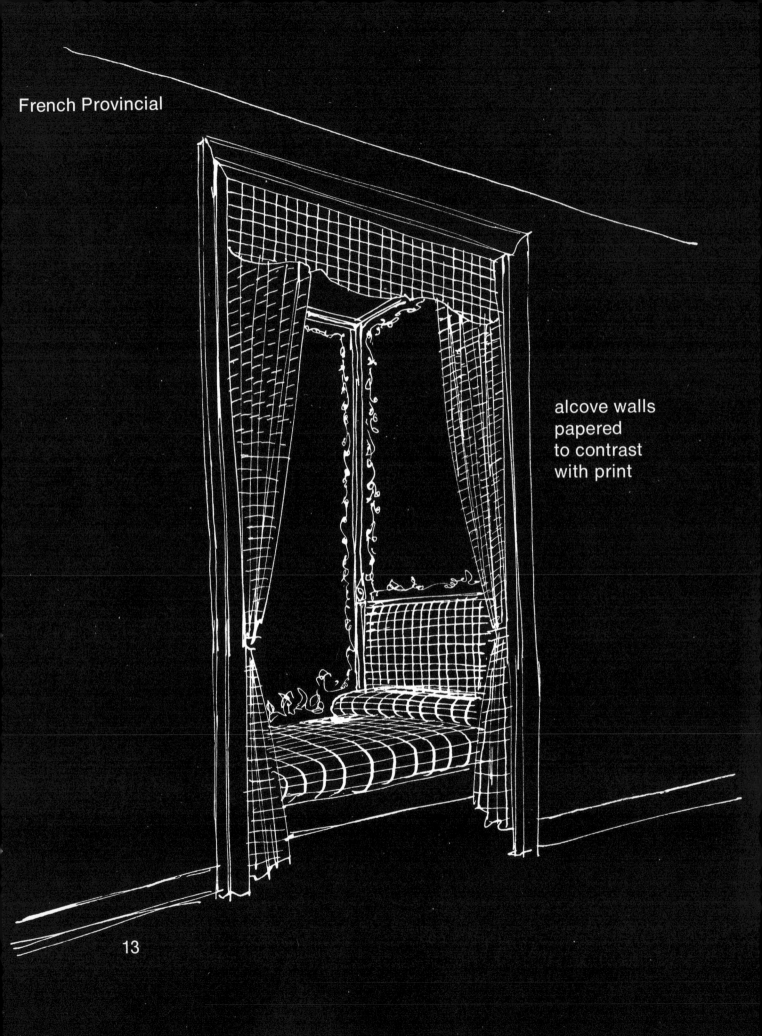

French Provincial

alcove walls
papered
to contrast
with print

13

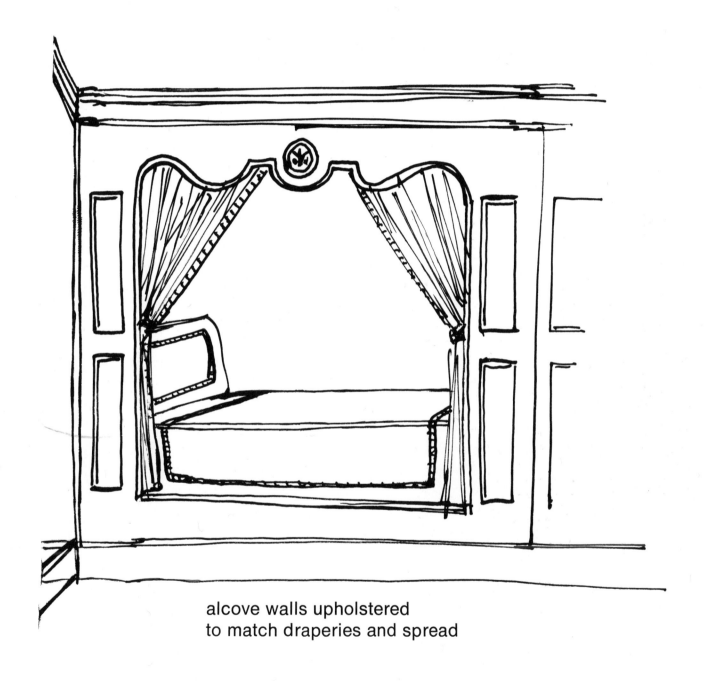

alcove walls upholstered
to match draperies and spread

15

Louis XVI

17

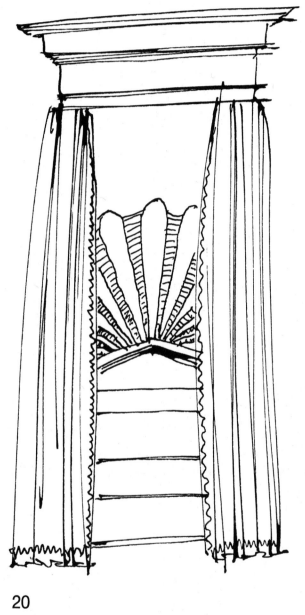

20

Louis XVI

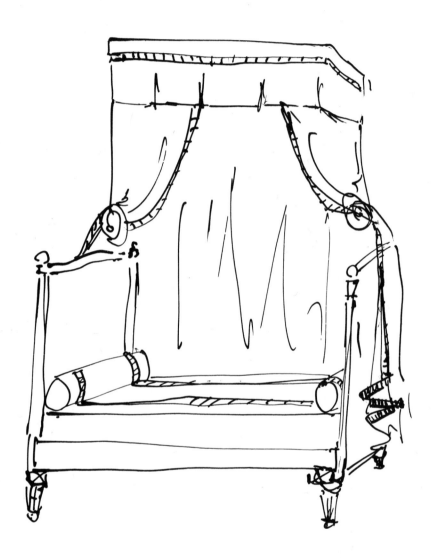

21

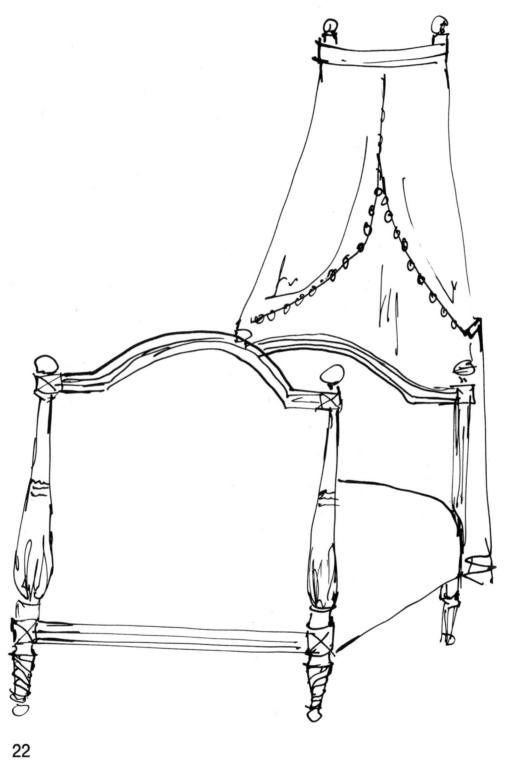

Louis XVI

half-canopy
with jabots

23

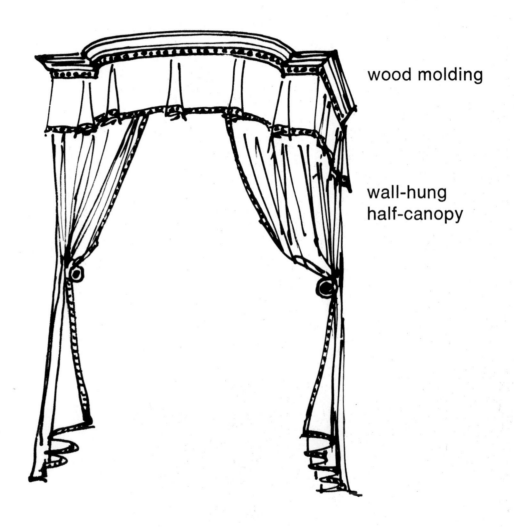

wood molding

wall-hung
half-canopy

24

Directoire

25

26

Empire

27

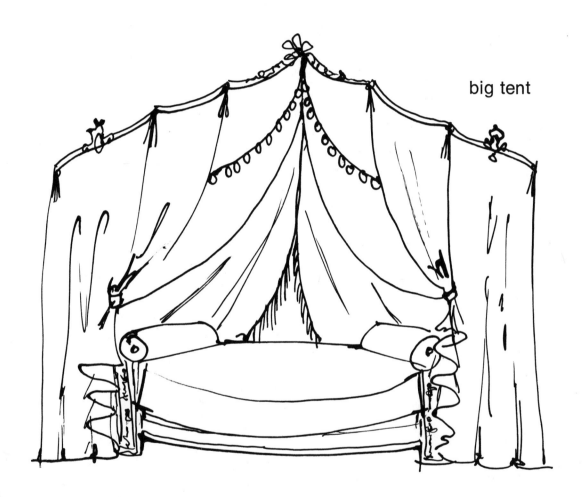

big tent

Empire

small tent

29

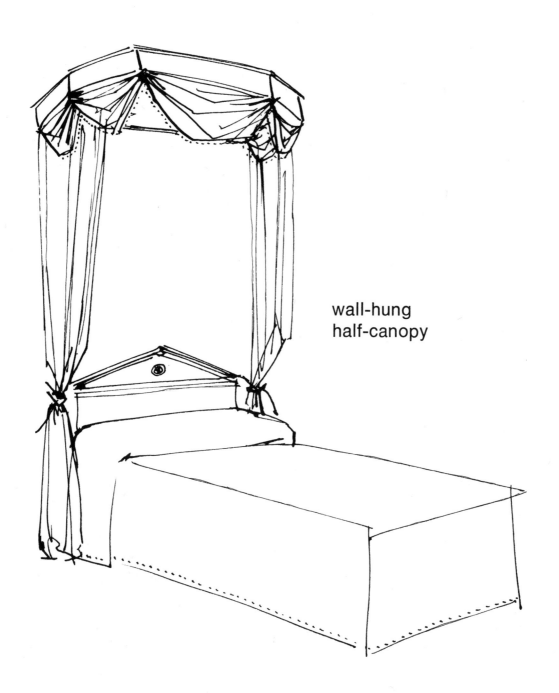

wall-hung
half-canopy

Empire

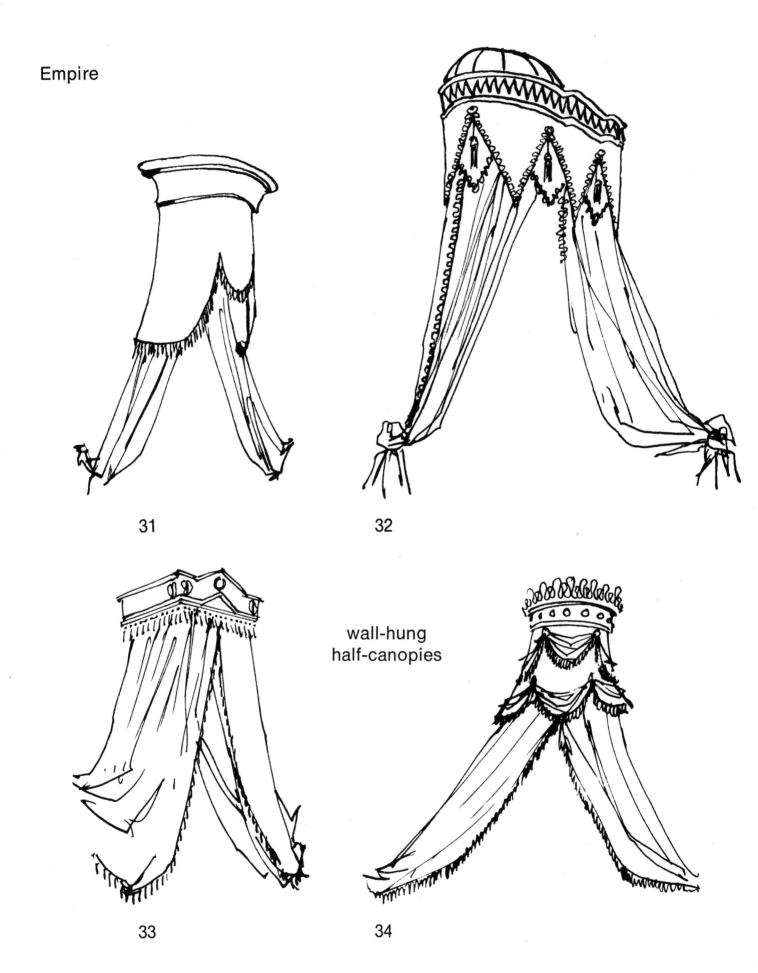

31

32

wall-hung
half-canopies

33

34

Queen Anne

Queen Anne

36

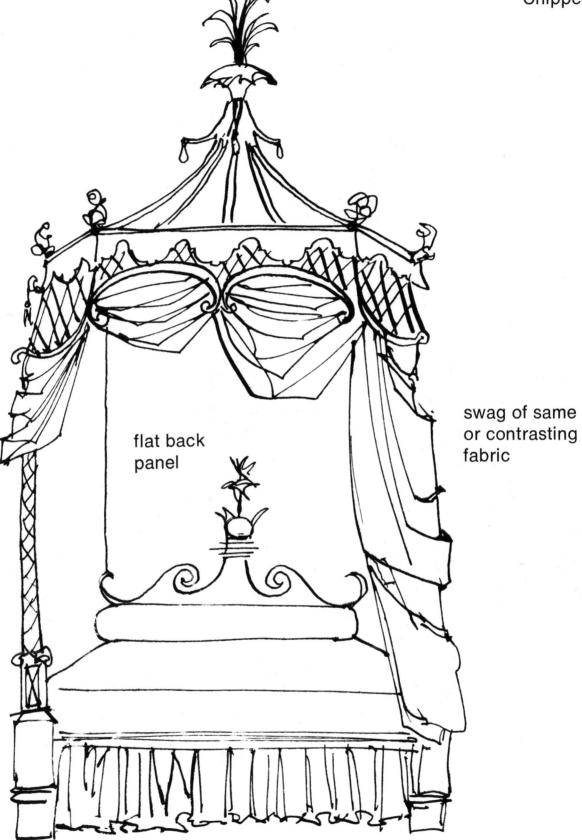

Chippendale

flat back
panel

swag of same
or contrasting
fabric

37

Chippendale

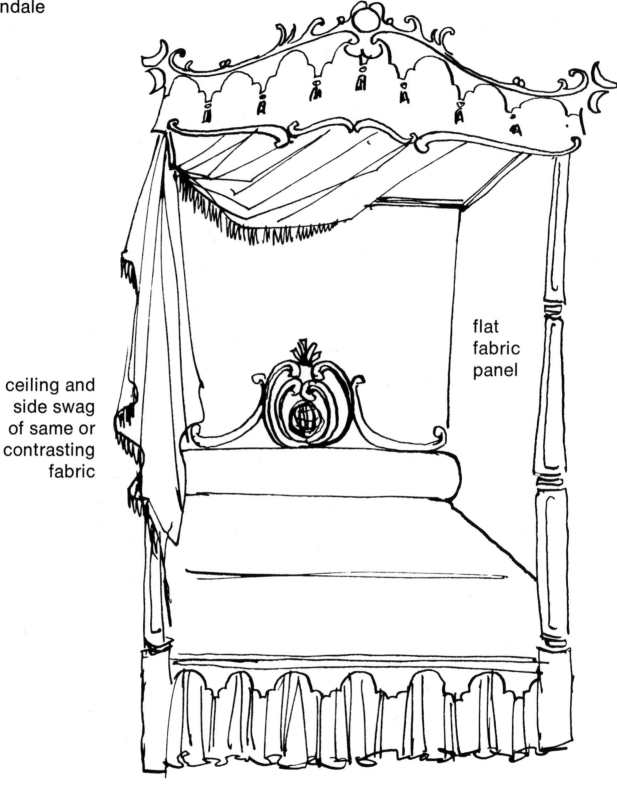

flat
fabric
panel

ceiling and
side swag
of same or
contrasting
fabric

38

shaped fabric
footdrop and
canopy

Chippendale

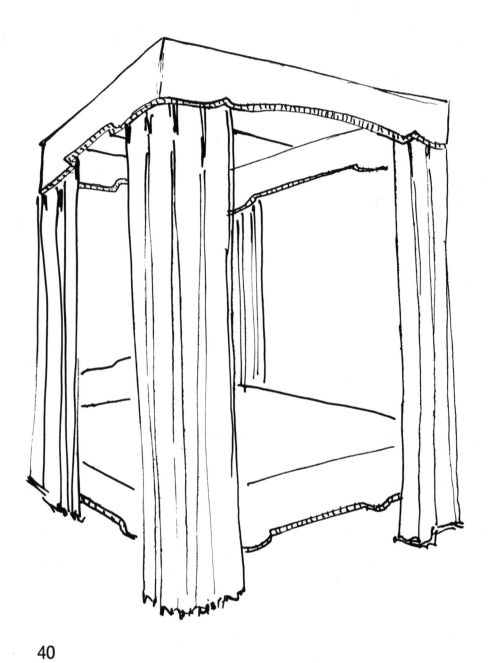

40

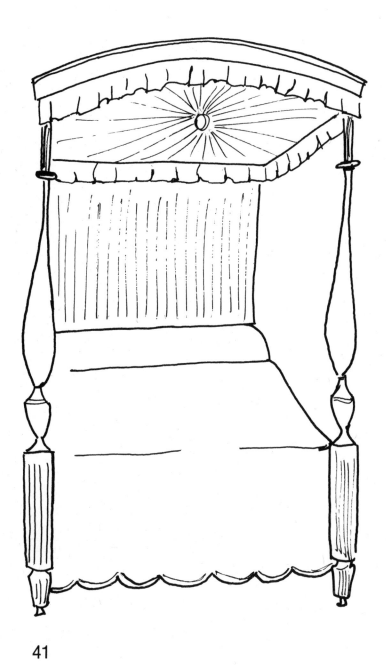

41

42

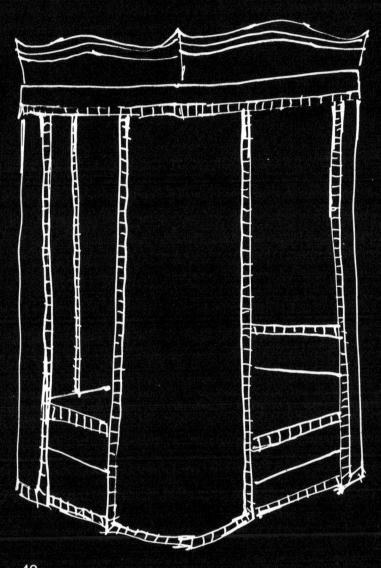

43

Victorian

shirred canopy,
striped valance

44

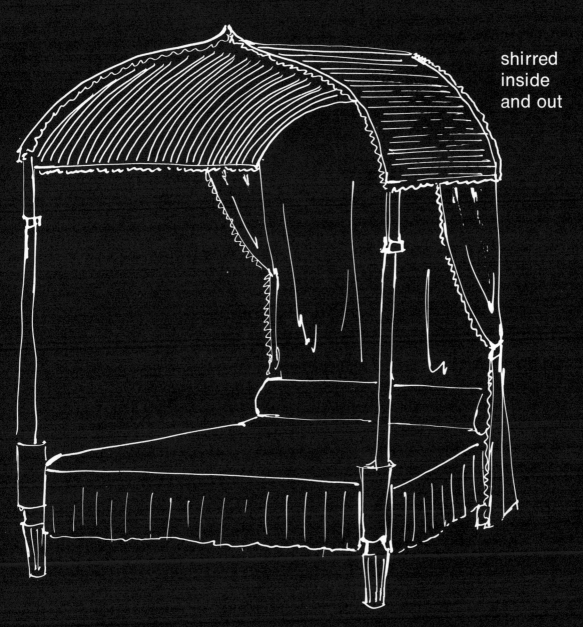

shirred
inside
and out

45

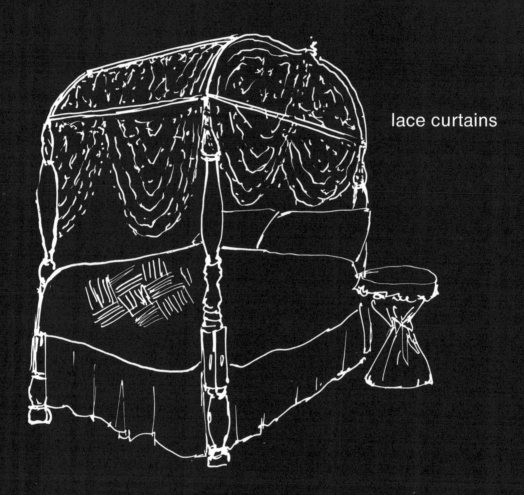

lace curtains

46

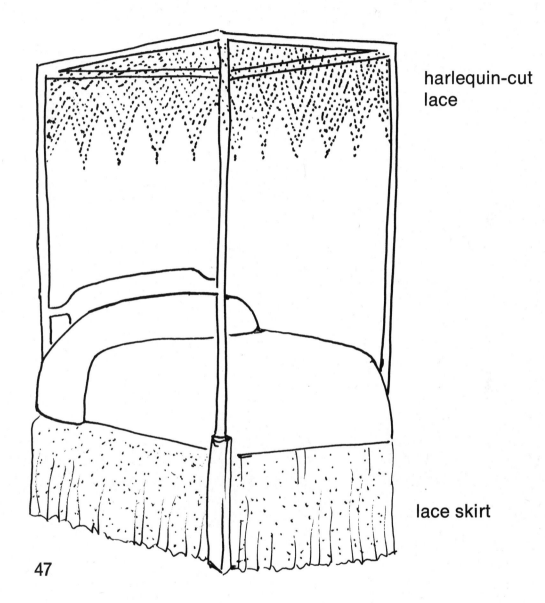

harlequin-cut
lace

lace skirt

47

lacy fabric veils
top of tester only—
slats show below

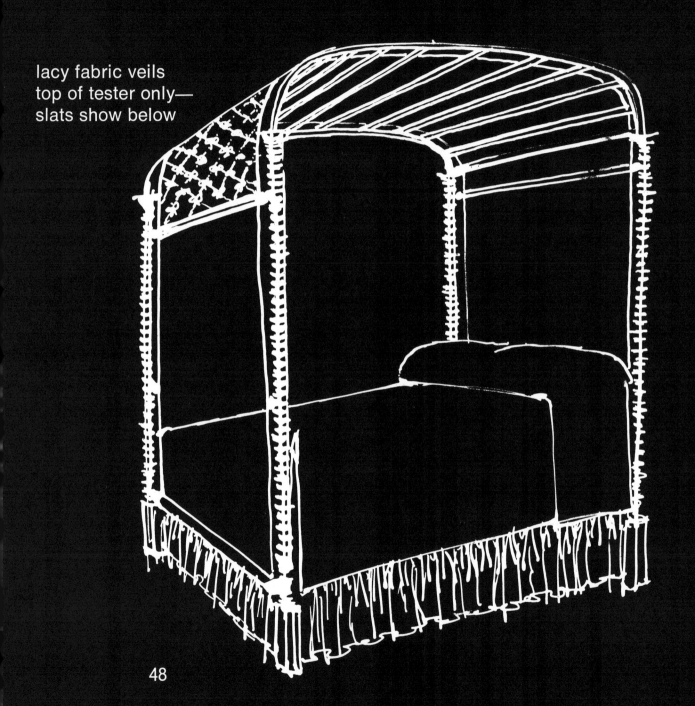

48

print outside,
plain inside

49

pleated tester

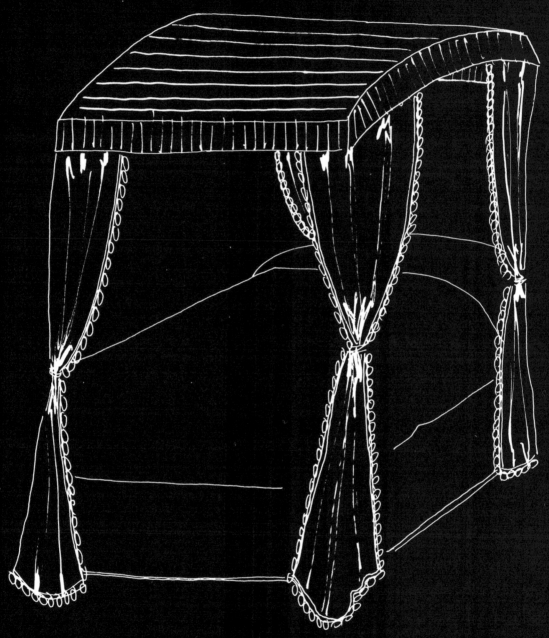

50

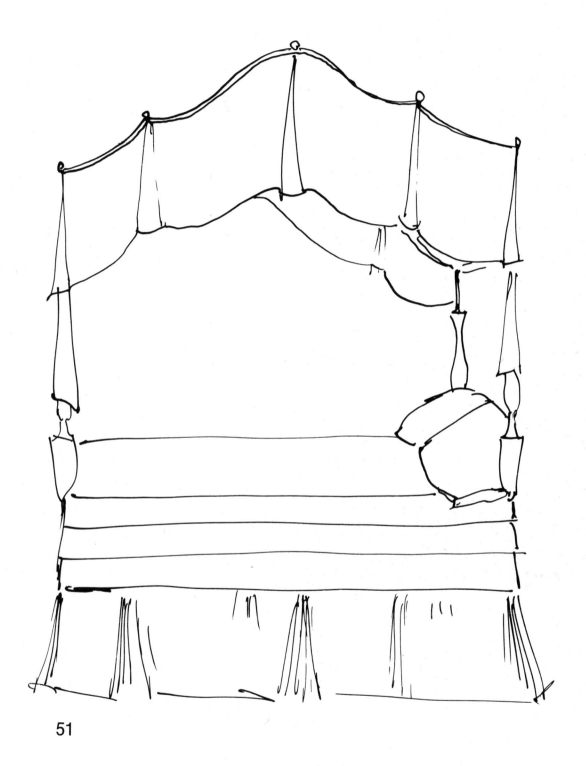

51

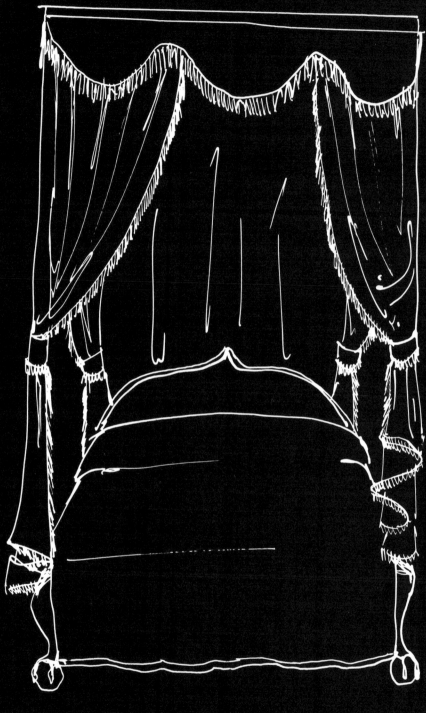

braid

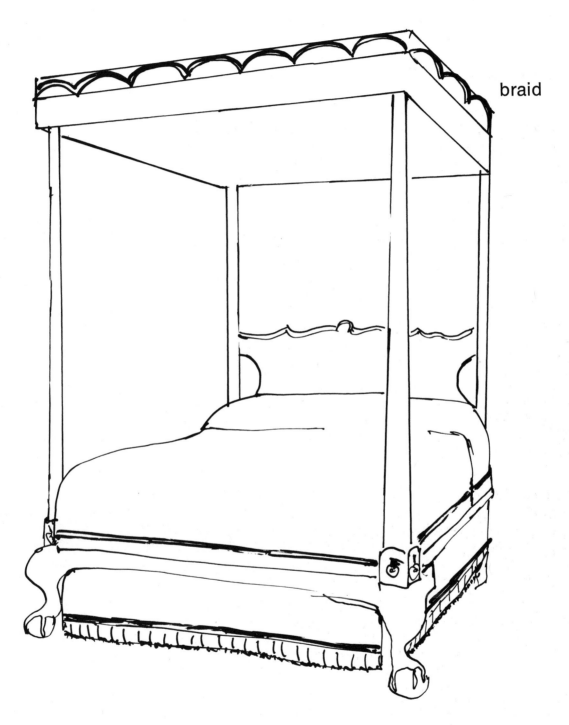

54

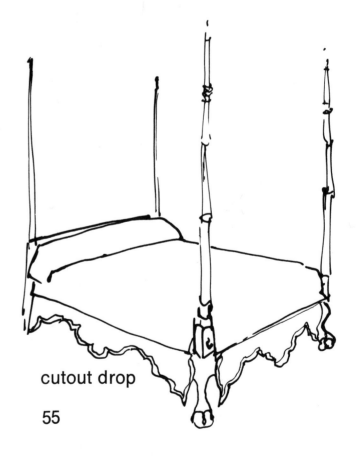

cutout drop

55

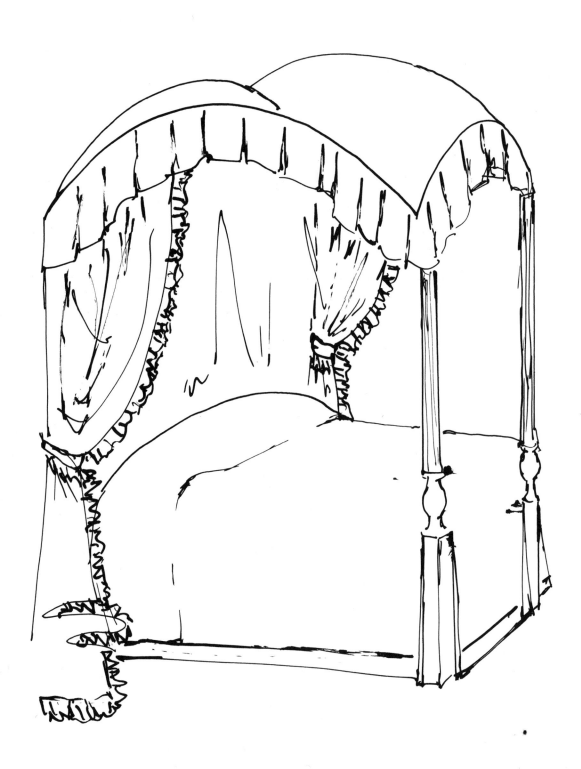

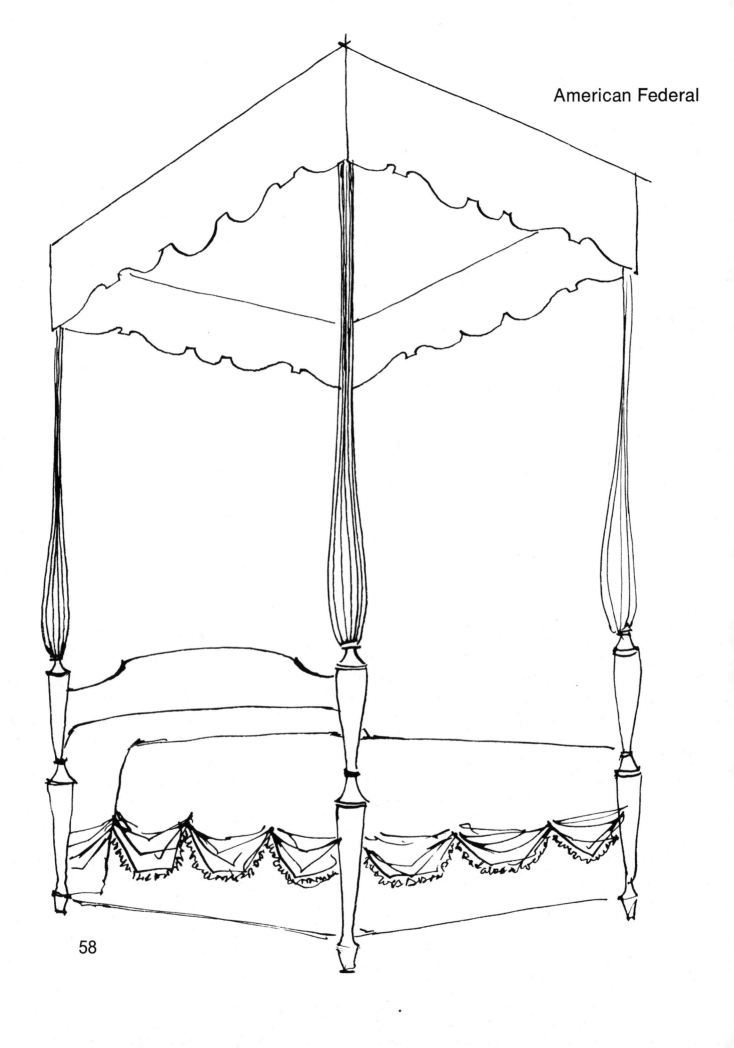

American Federal

58

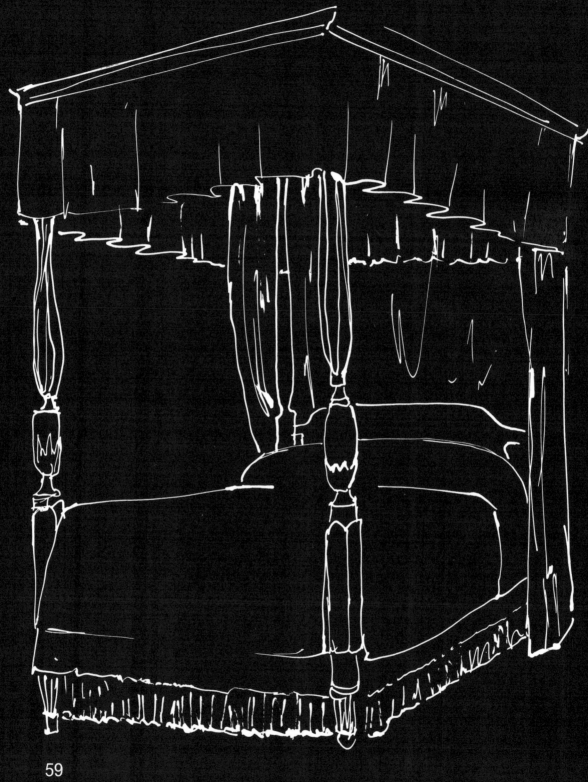

American Federal

61

62

formal designs

63

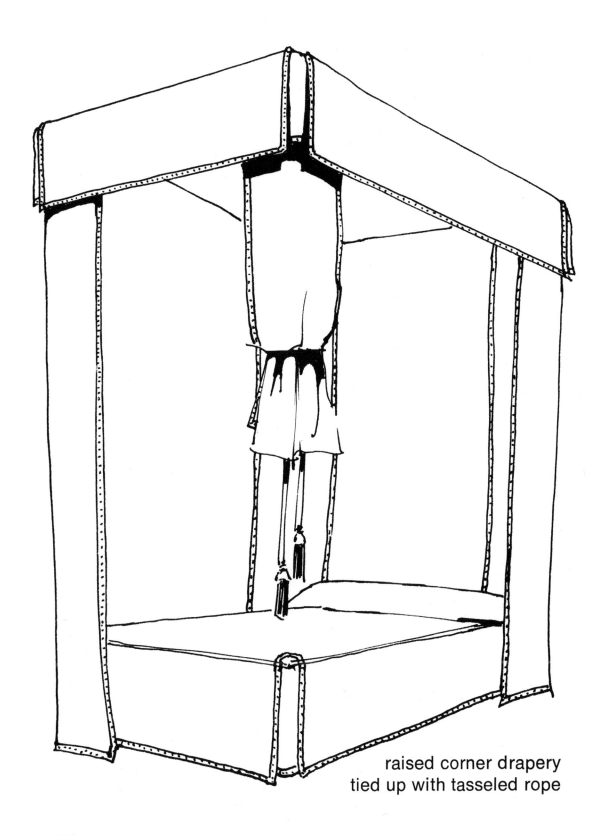

raised corner drapery
tied up with tasseled rope

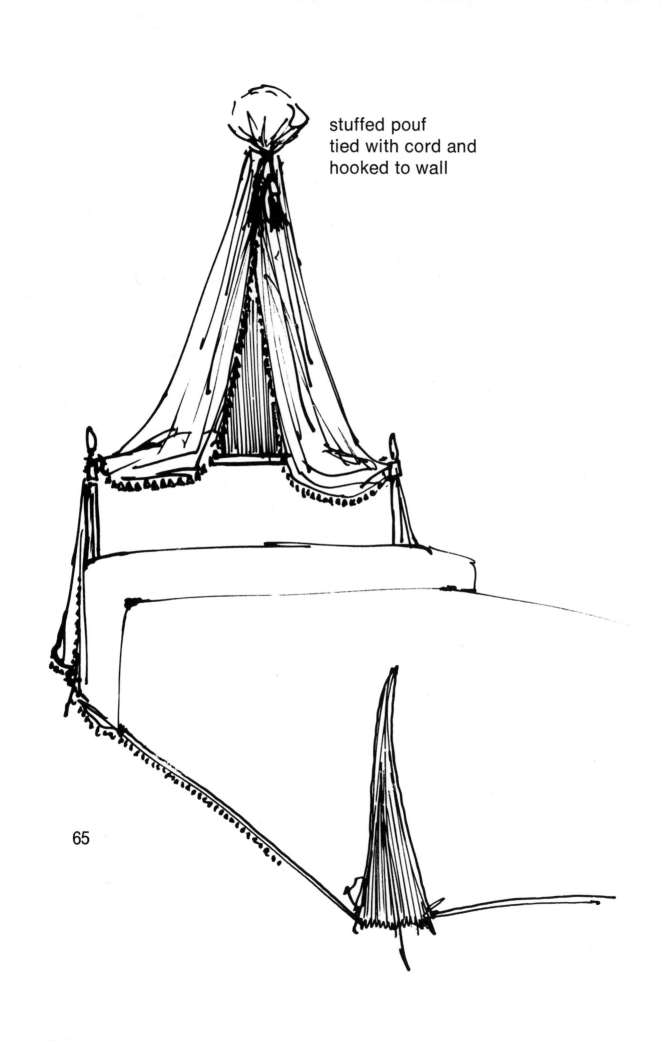

stuffed pouf
tied with cord and
hooked to wall

65

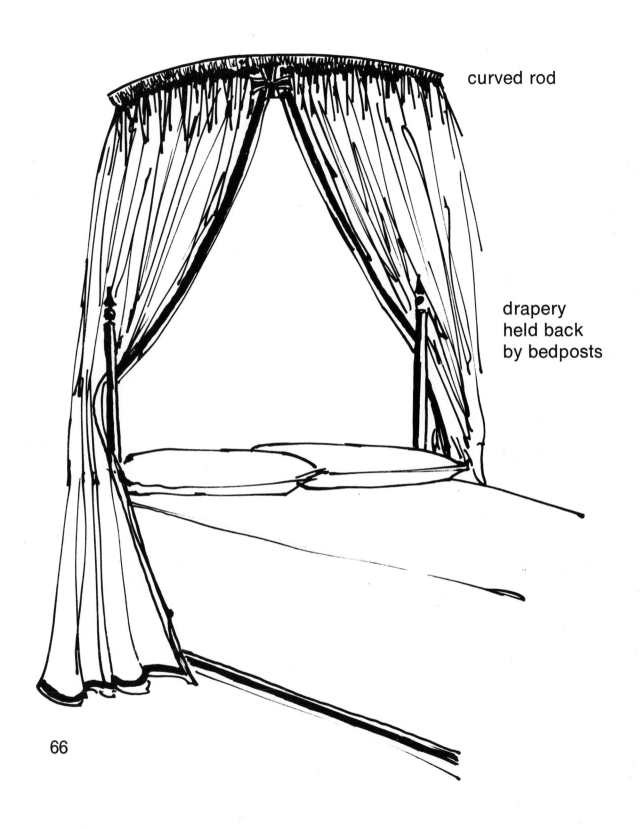

curved rod

drapery
held back
by bedposts

66

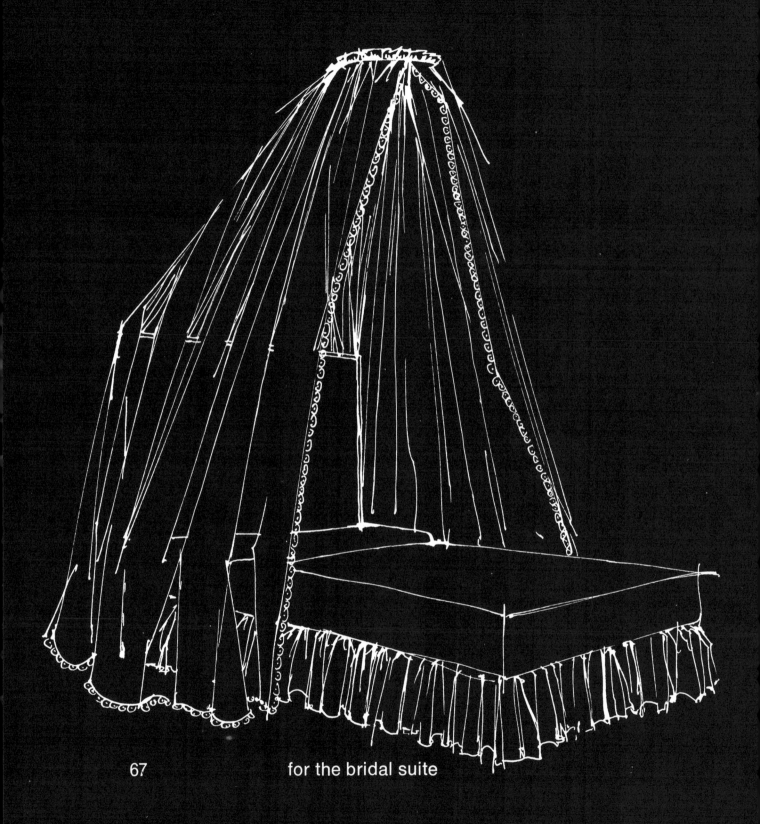

67   for the bridal suite

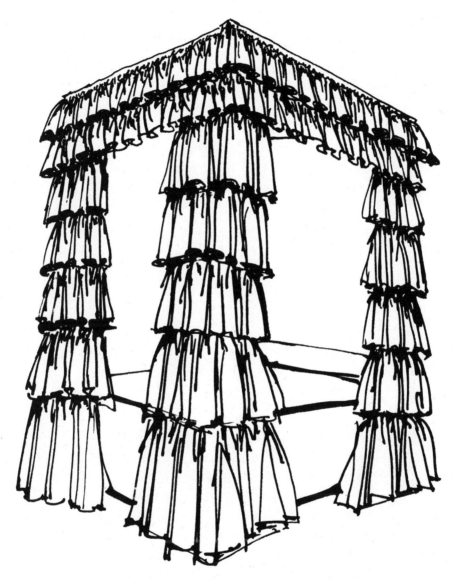

graduating ruffles

poufs tied
to hidden posts

69

70

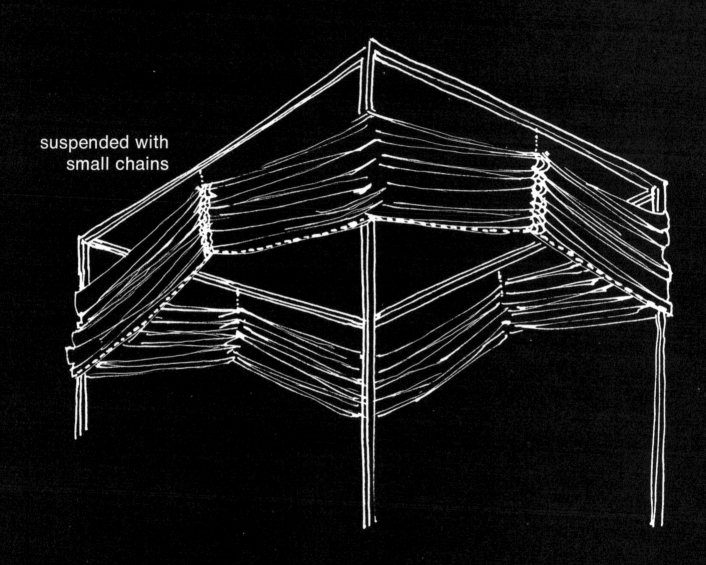

suspended with
small chains

71

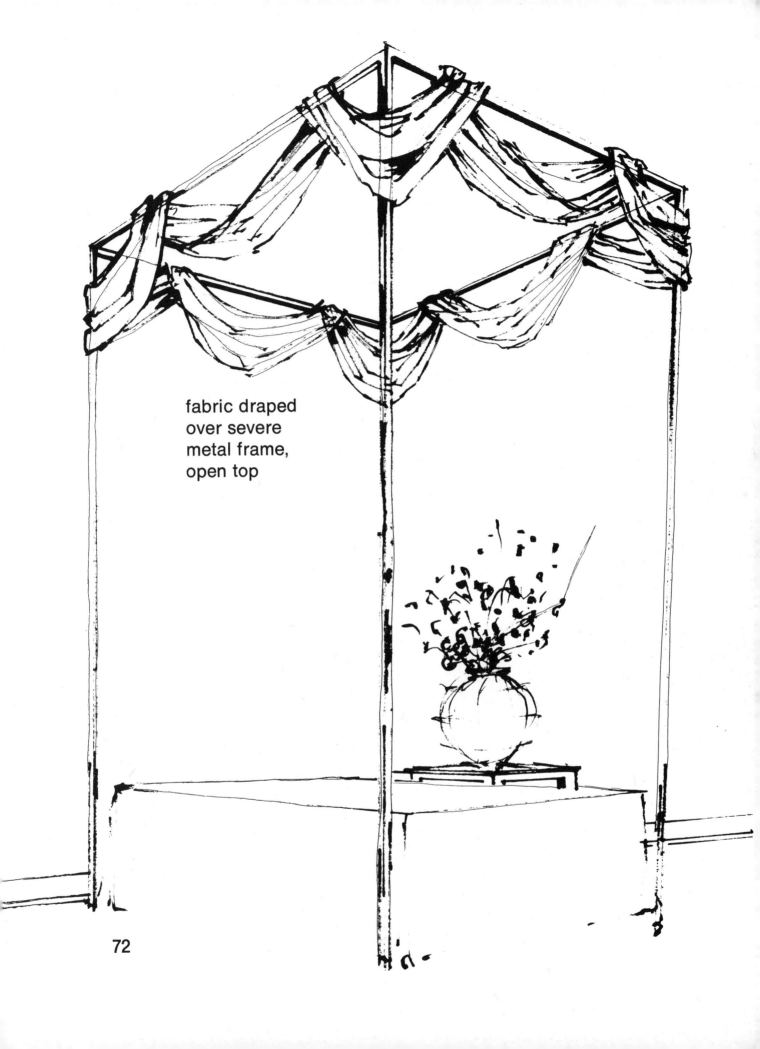

fabric draped
over severe
metal frame,
open top

72

73

74

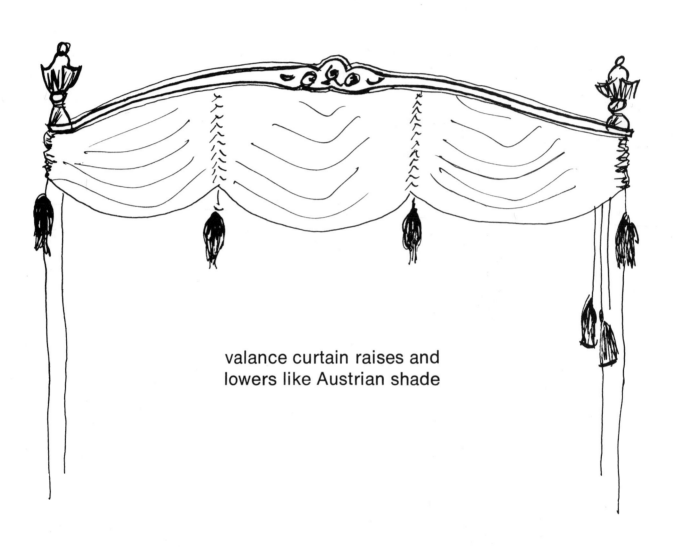

valance curtain raises and
lowers like Austrian shade

75

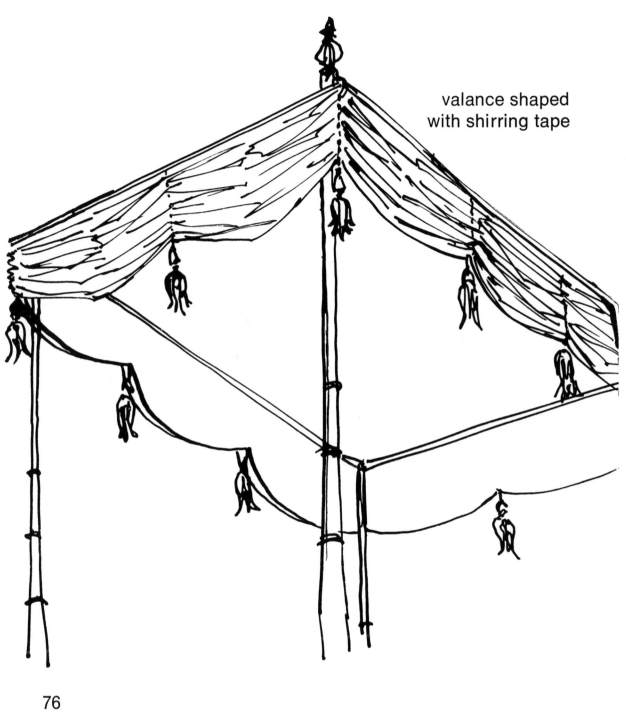

valance shaped
with shirring tape

76

77

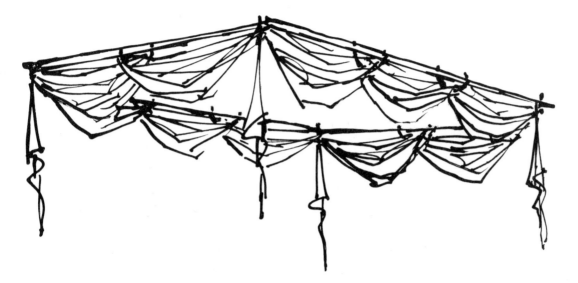

canopy attached to ceiling

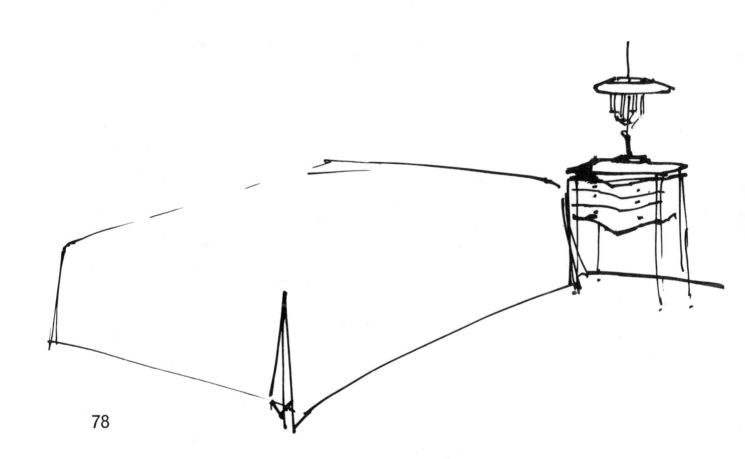

78

rod flanged
to wall

79

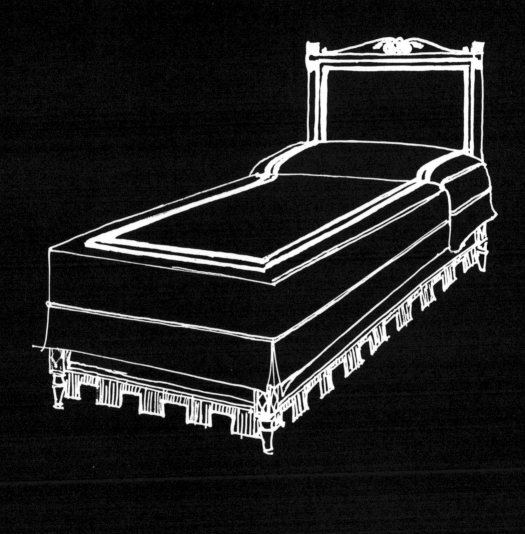

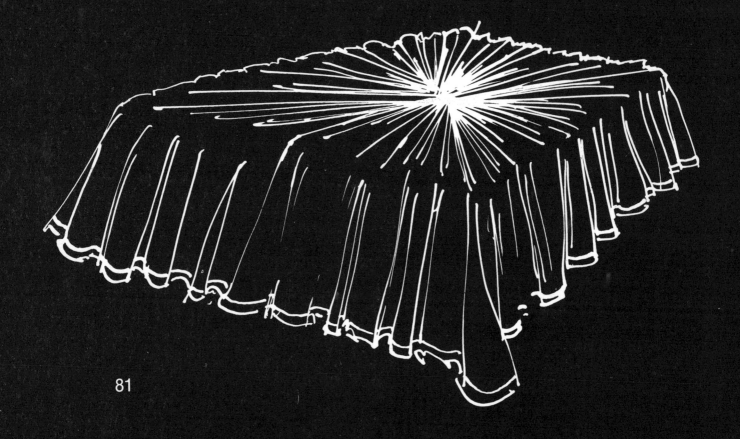

81

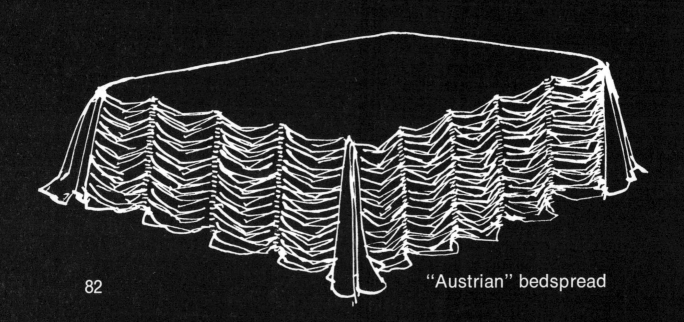

82

"Austrian" bedspread

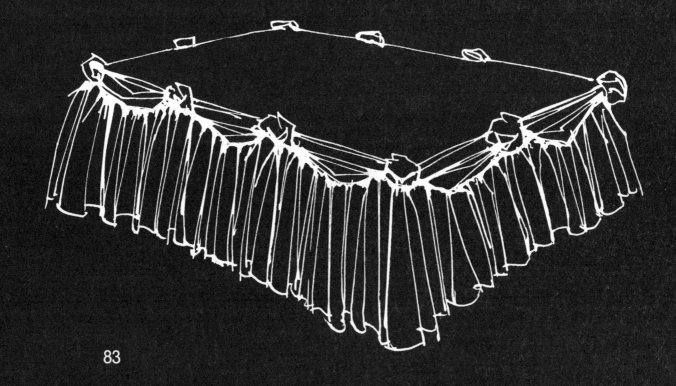

83

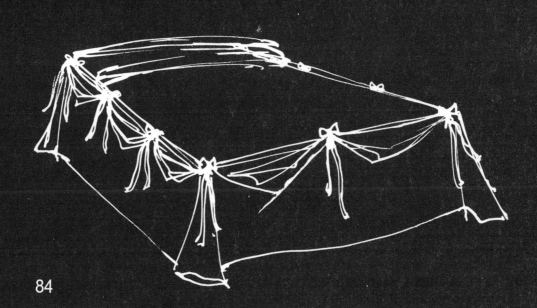

84

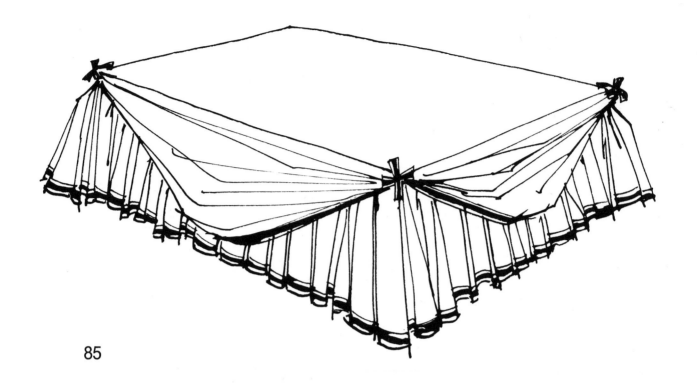

85

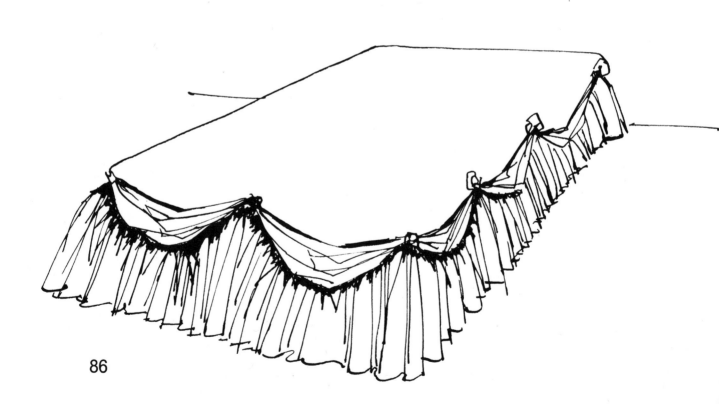

86

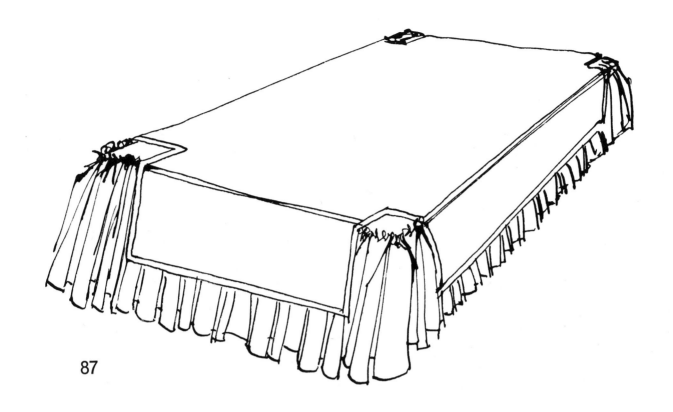

87

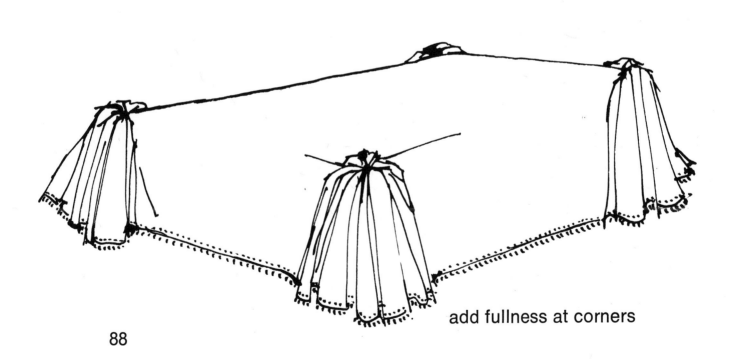

add fullness at corners

88

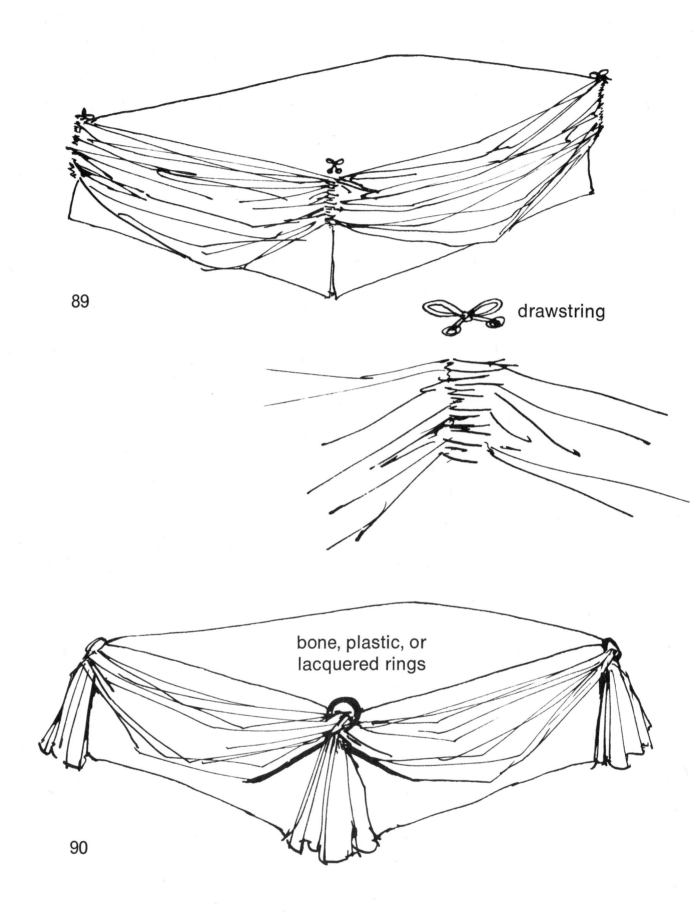

89

drawstring

bone, plastic, or
lacquered rings

90

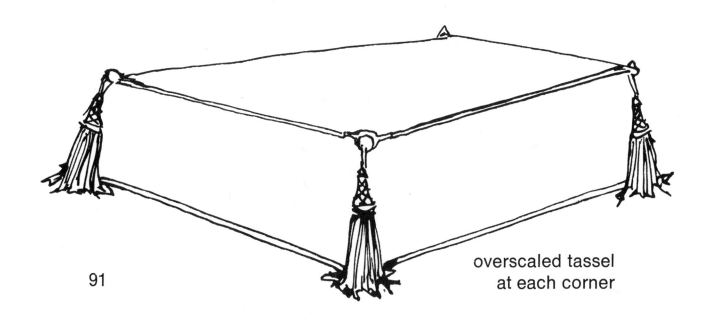

91

overscaled tassel
at each corner

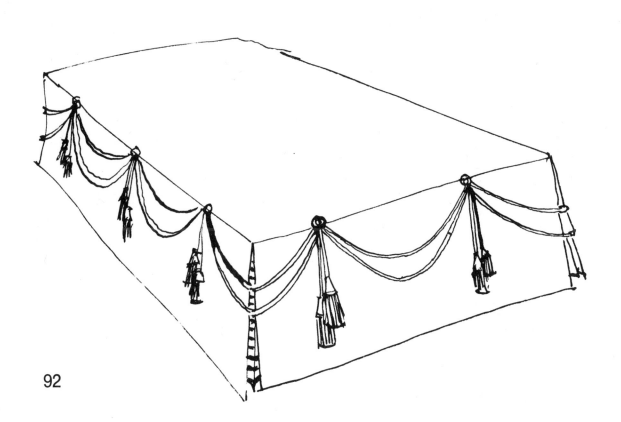

92

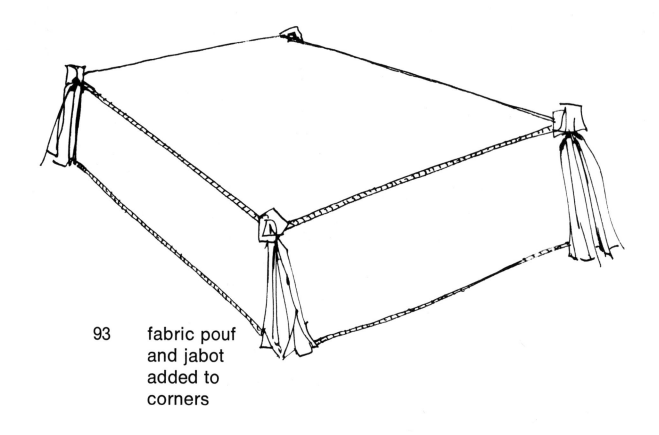

93   fabric pouf
      and jabot
      added to
      corners

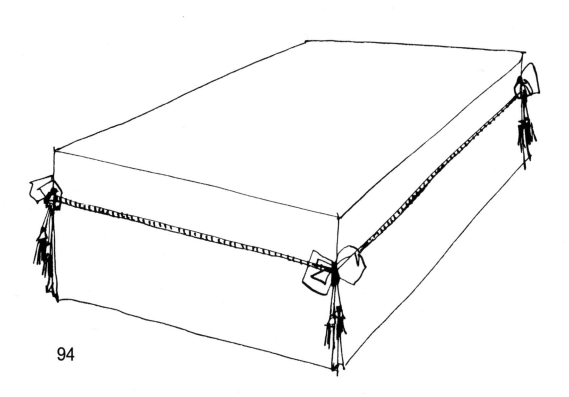

94

95

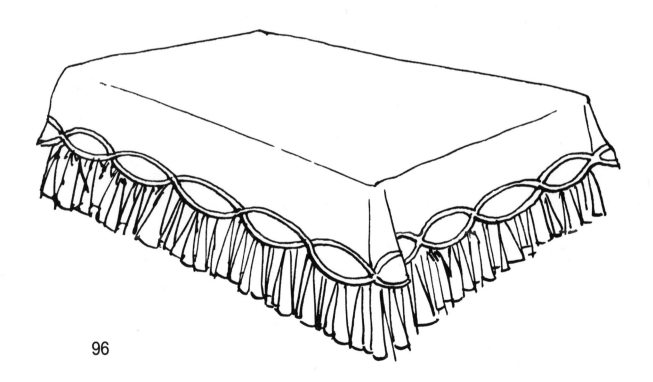

96

97

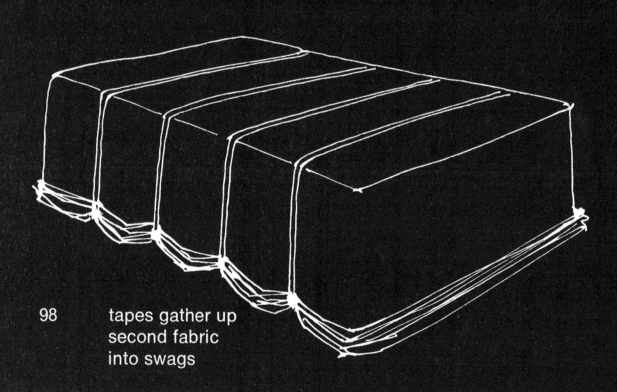

98   tapes gather up
second fabric
into swags

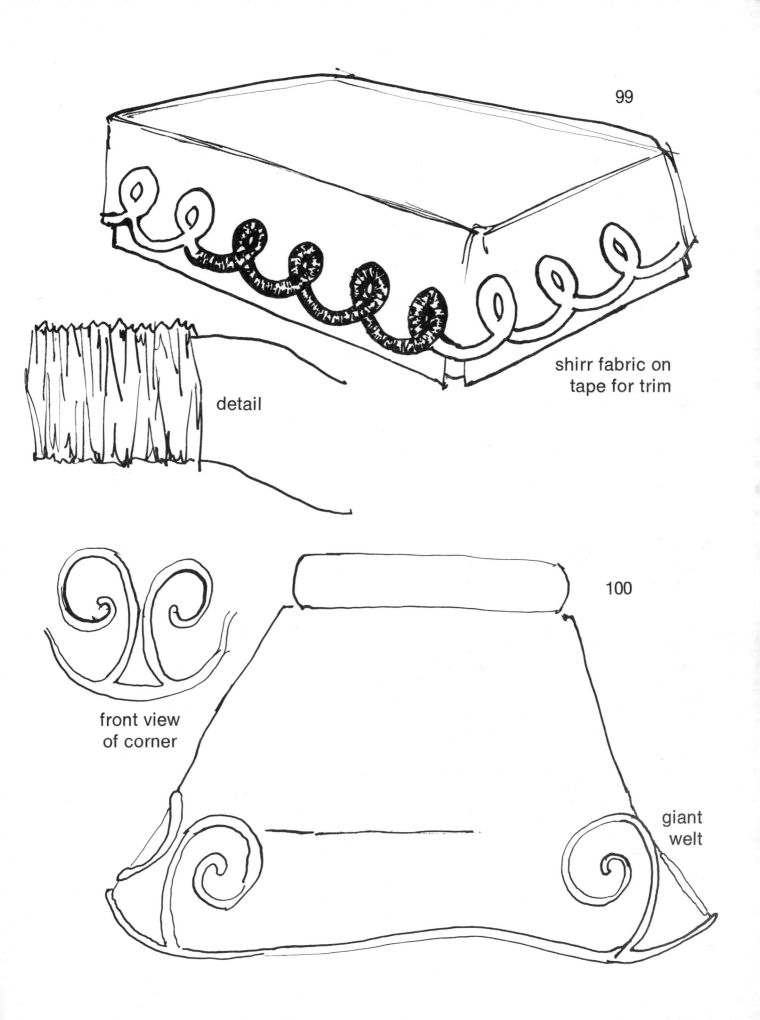

99

shirr fabric on
tape for trim

detail

front view
of corner

100

giant
welt

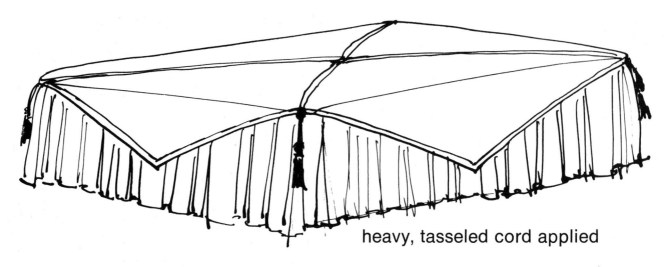

heavy, tasseled cord applied

101

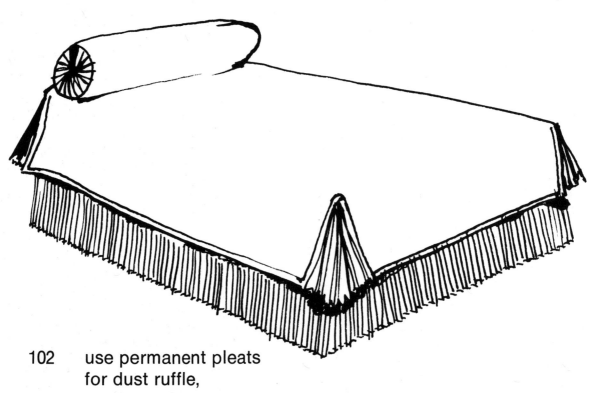

102   use permanent pleats
for dust ruffle,
for ends of bolster,
and at corners of spread

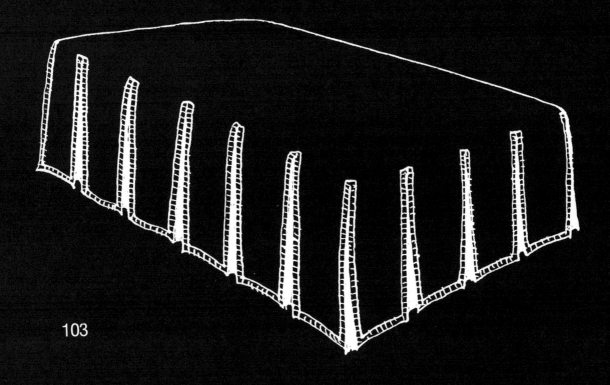

103

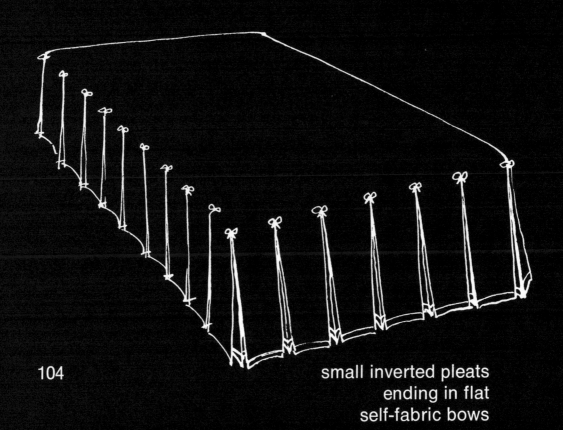

104

small inverted pleats
ending in flat
self-fabric bows

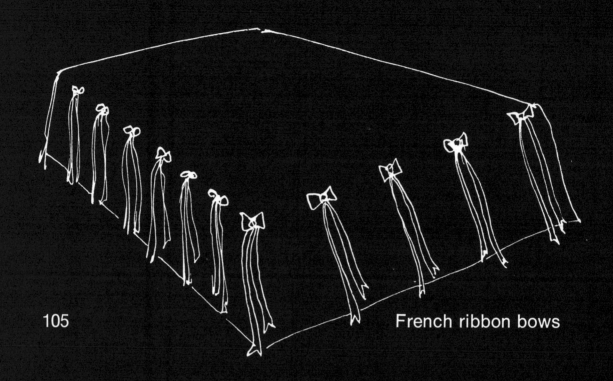

105   French ribbon bows

apply braid
in fancy design

106

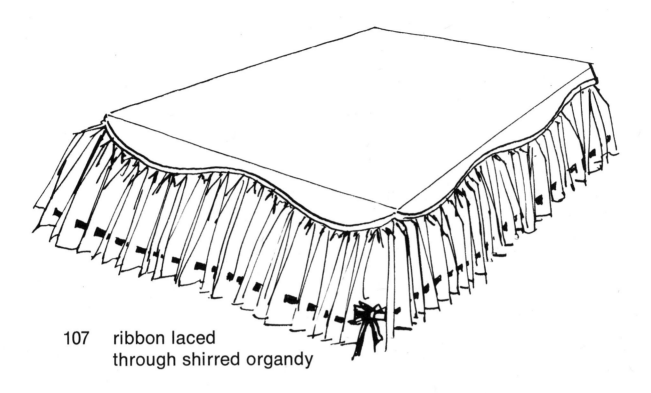

107   ribbon laced
through shirred organdy

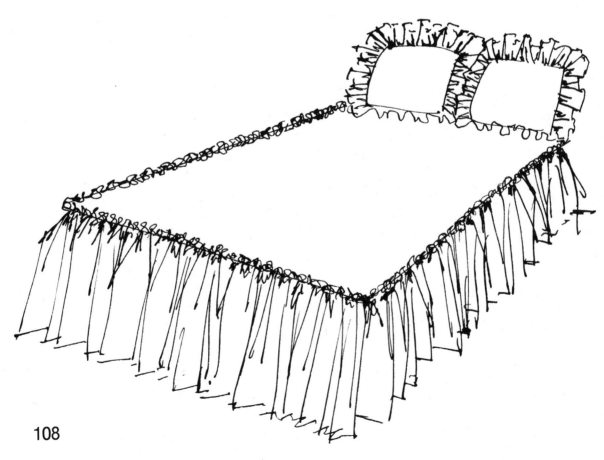

108

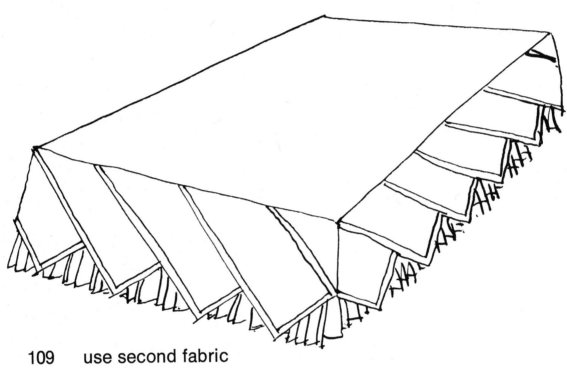

109   use second fabric
for petal binding
and skirt

casual
designs

oval rod mounted to ceiling

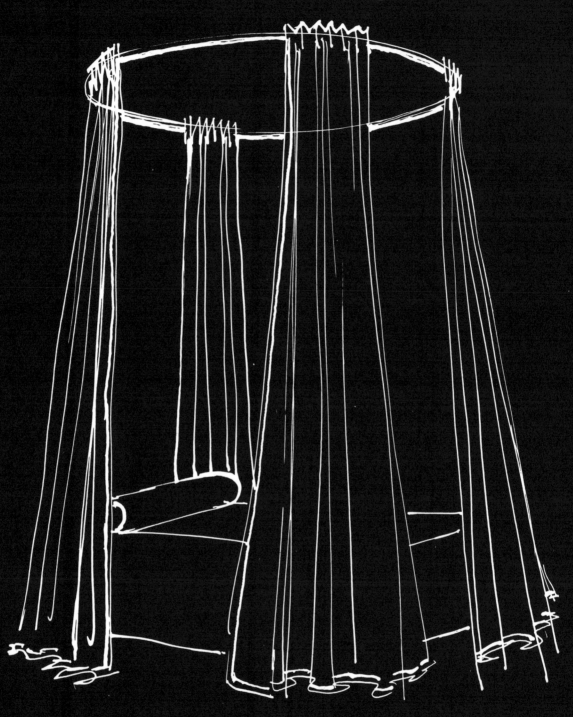

wooden frame
with fabric ceiling
trimmed
with braid

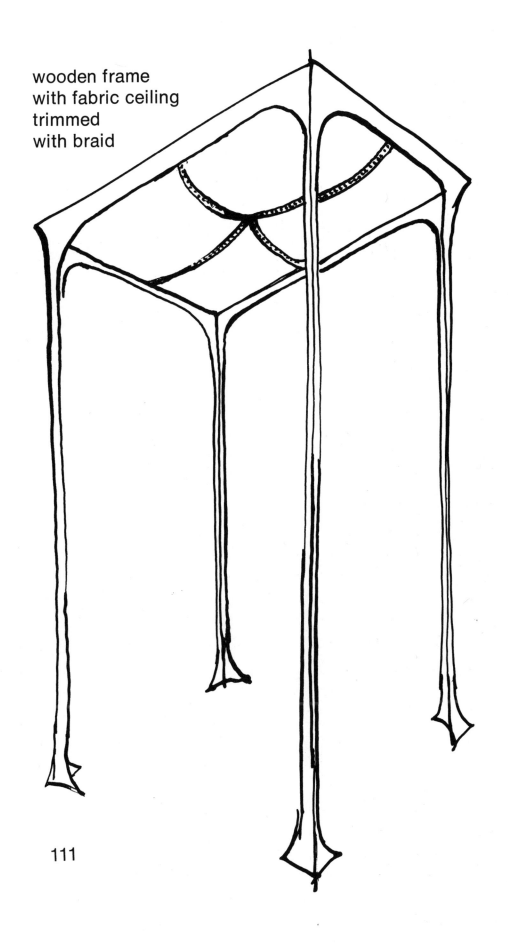

111

twin beds under one canopy

112

trimming tape over
striped fabric

flaps folded
back like
a tent

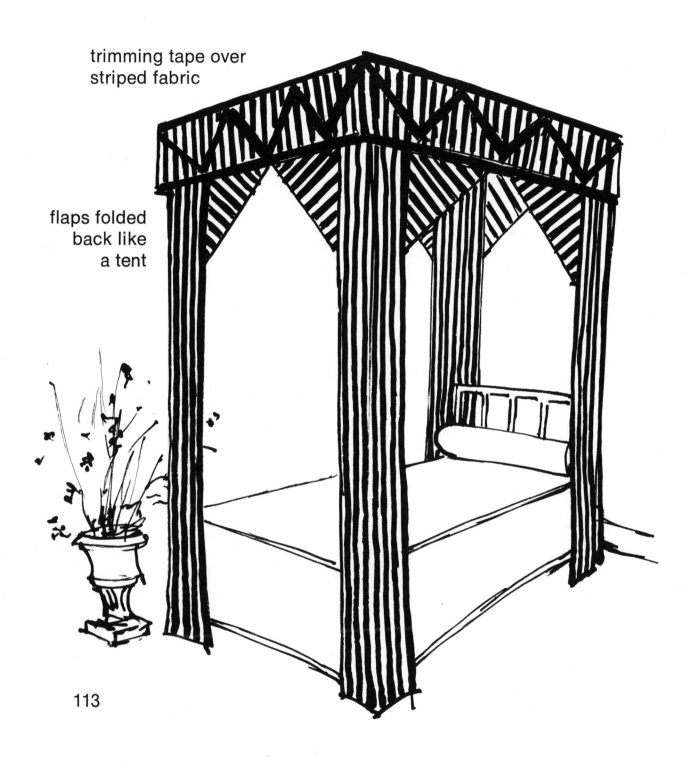

113

114

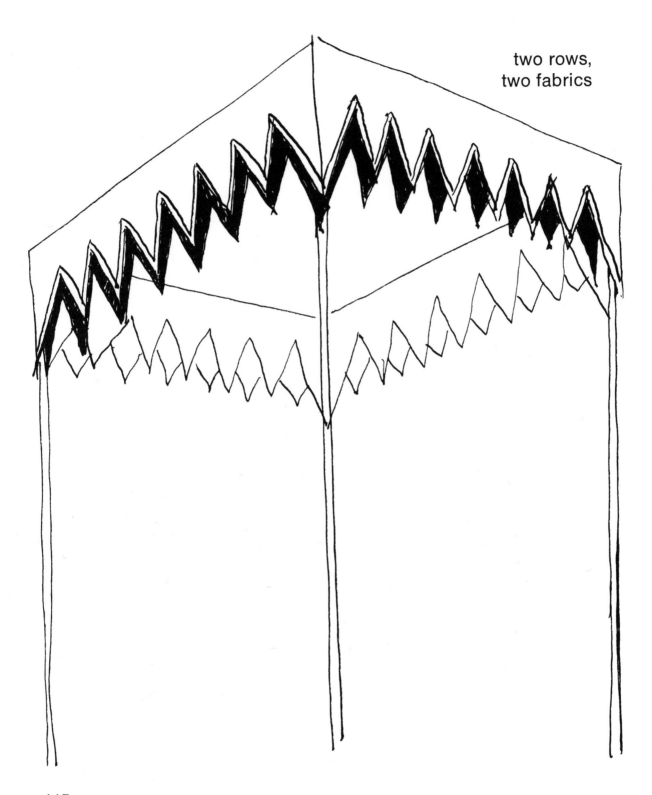

two rows,
two fabrics

115

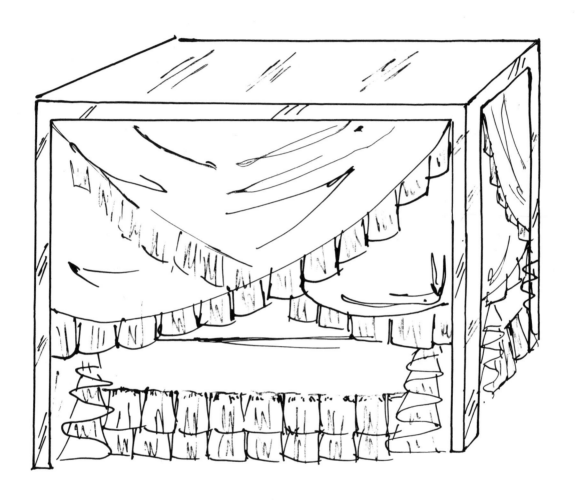

116   organdy curtains with severe steel frame

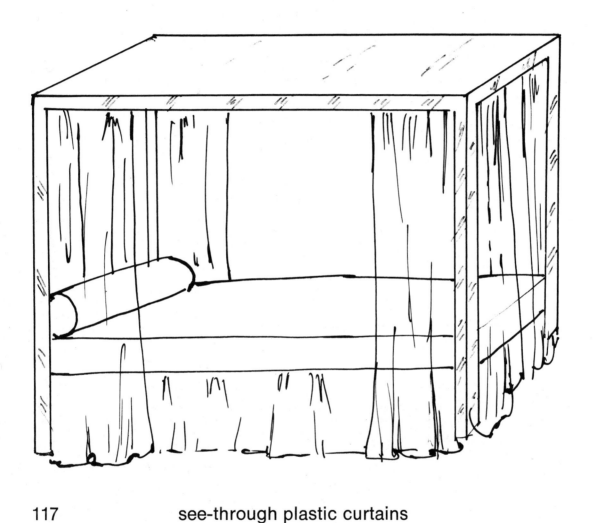

117   see-through plastic curtains
with severe steel frame

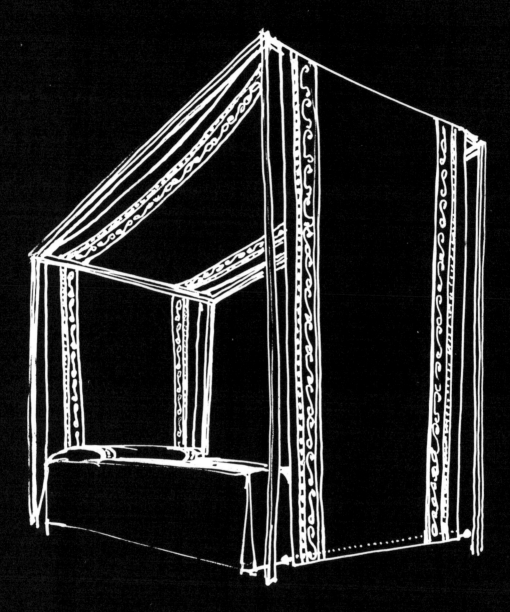

118   trim applied to plain panel

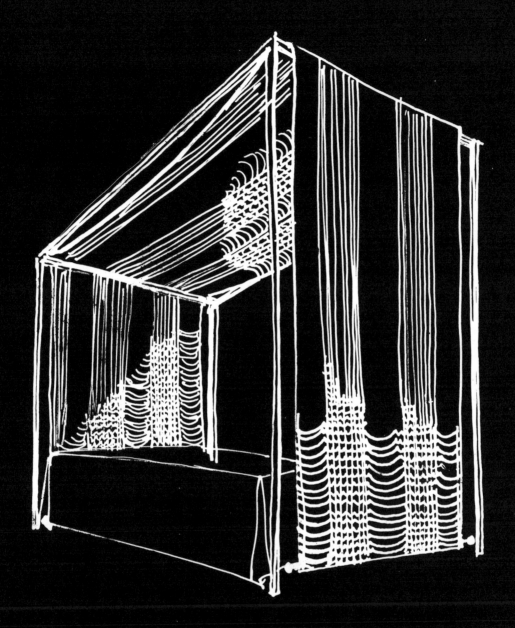

119   casement tent

tabs at top
and bottom

120   more tabs

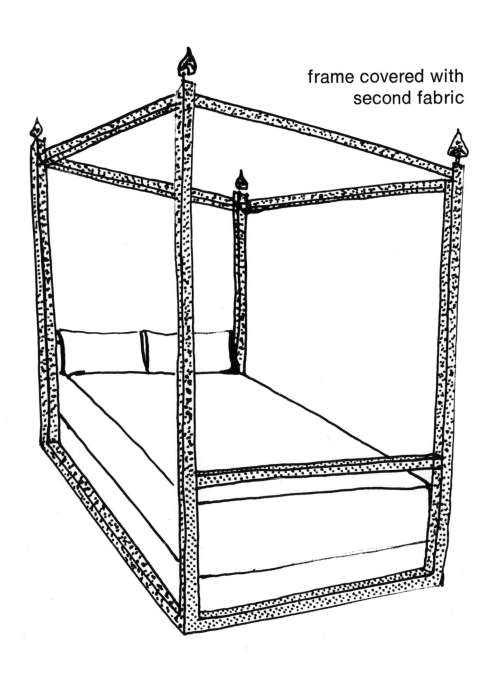

frame covered with
second fabric

poles and canopy attach
to ceiling and base platform—
border canopy does not
cover entire ceiling

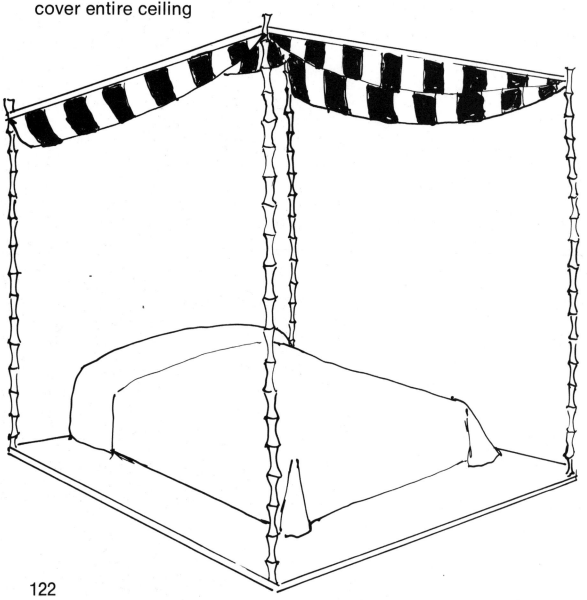

122

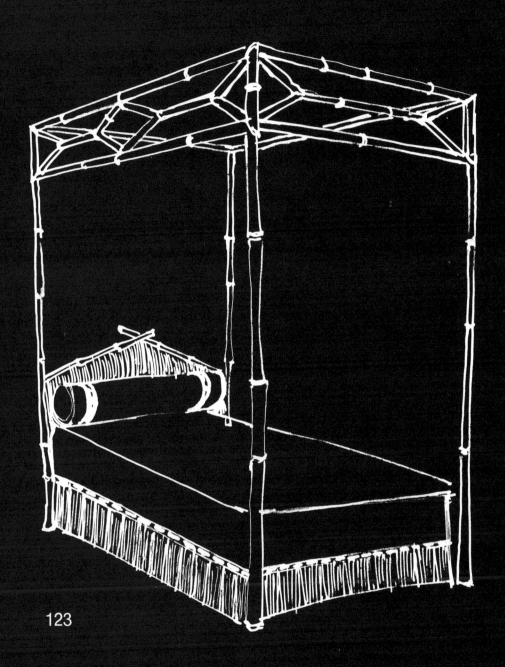

123

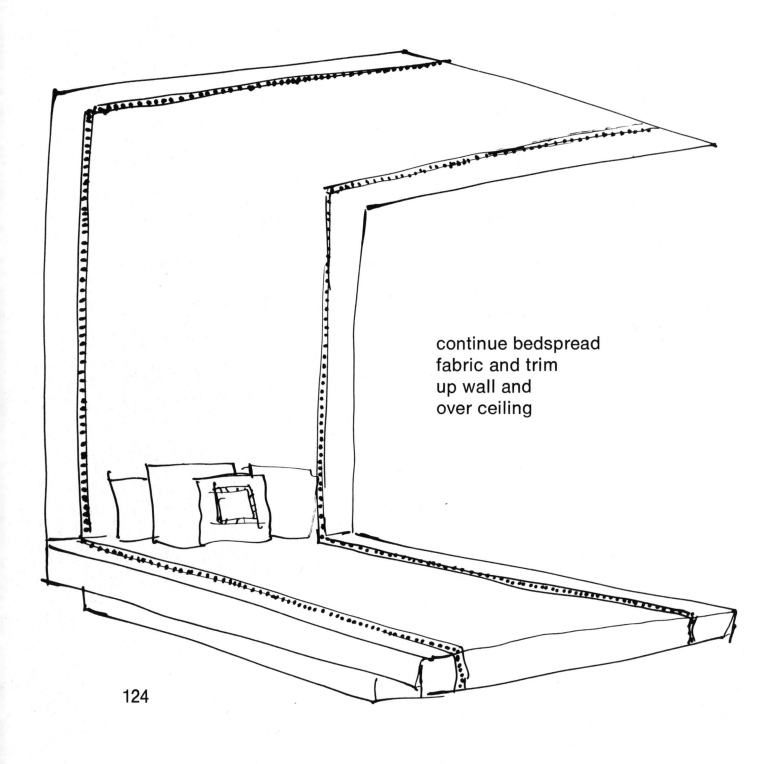

continue bedspread
fabric and trim
up wall and
over ceiling

124

saris or bordered provincial print
for valance, folded pelmets, and bedspread

stiffened canopy
hung by ring
from ceiling

126

fabric valance
and draperies
create bed alcove
at end of room

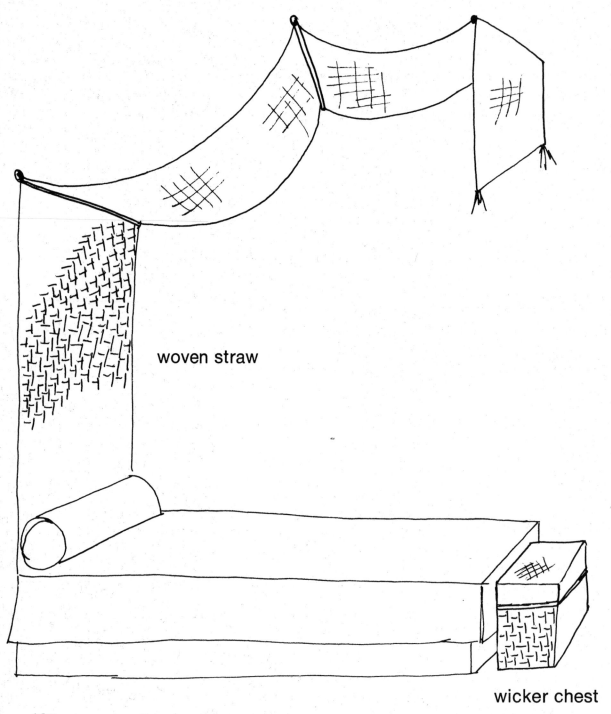

woven straw

wicker chest

128

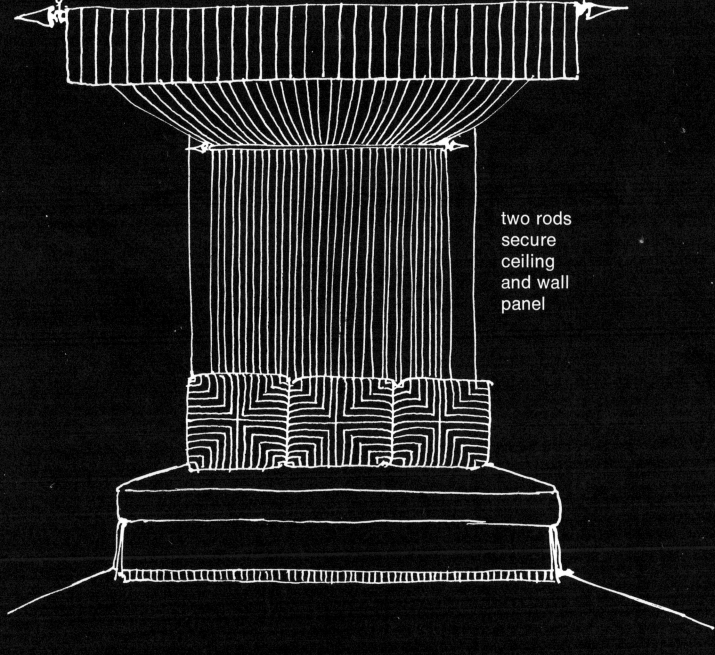

two rods
secure
ceiling
and wall
panel

129

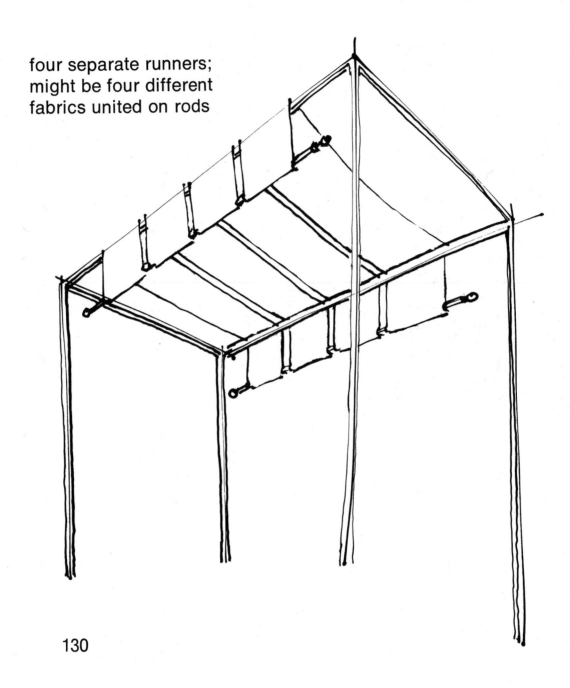

four separate runners;
might be four different
fabrics united on rods

130

fabric runners lined
with contrasting color
or pattern and basket-woven
over canopy frame

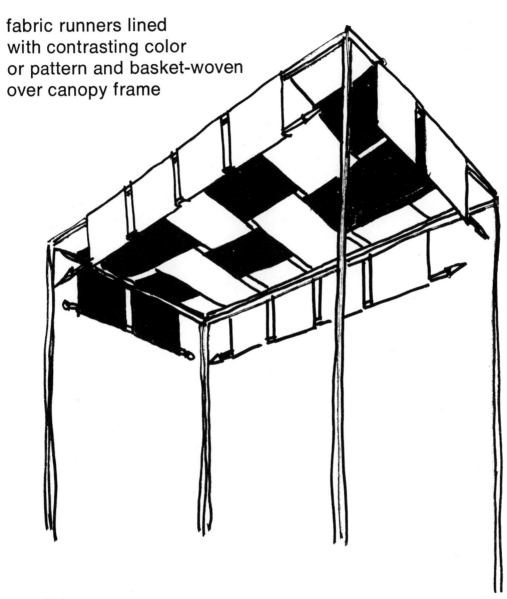

131

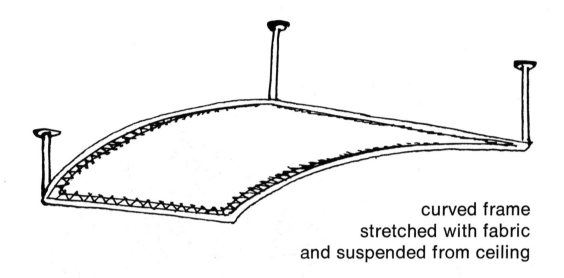

curved frame
stretched with fabric
and suspended from ceiling

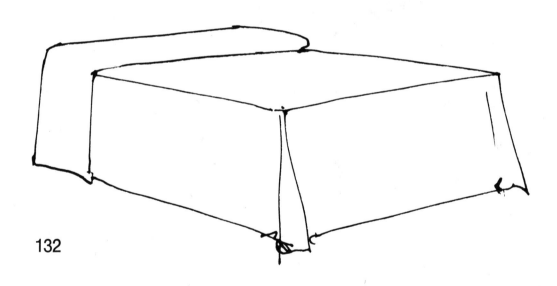

132

Austrian canopy
and curtains
following dormer line

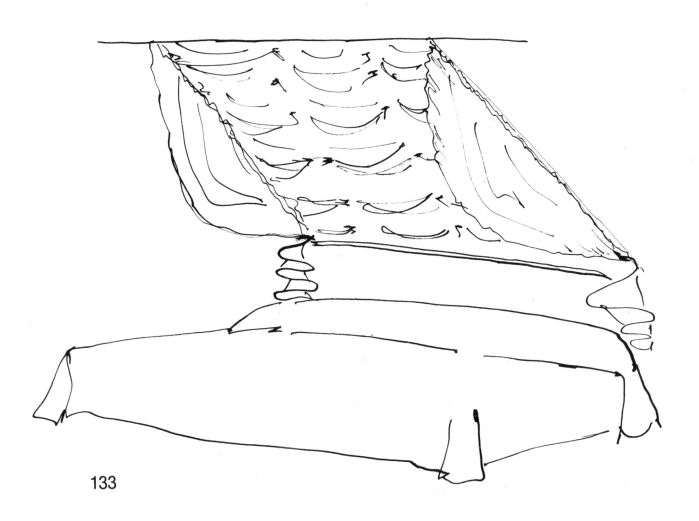

133

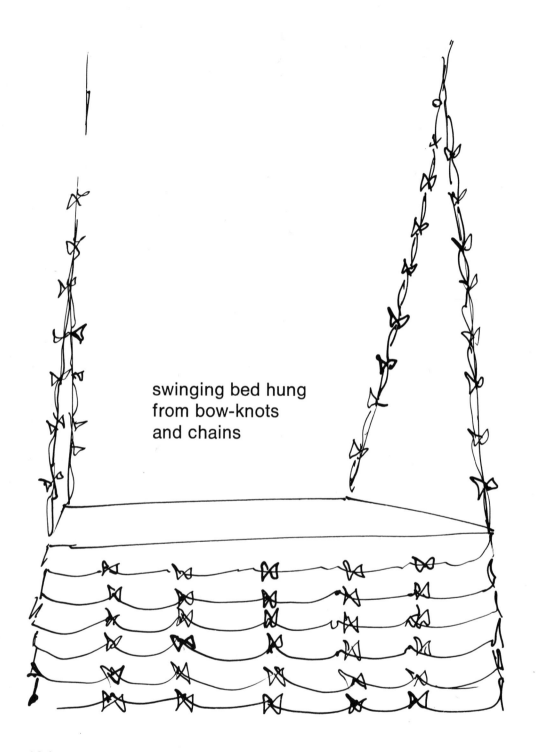

swinging bed hung
from bow-knots
and chains

134   bows on ruffled skirt

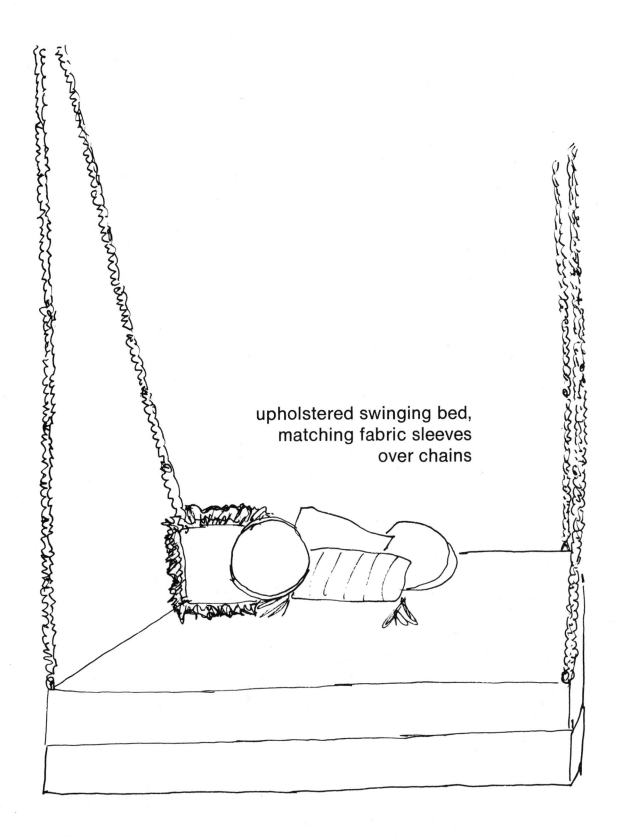

upholstered swinging bed,
matching fabric sleeves
over chains

135

136

137   corner tassels on a fitted spread

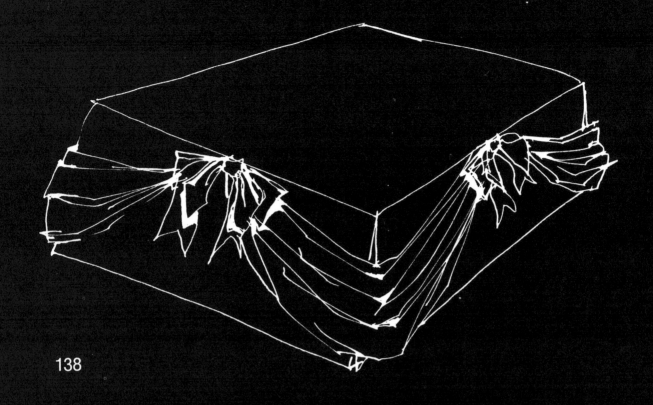

138

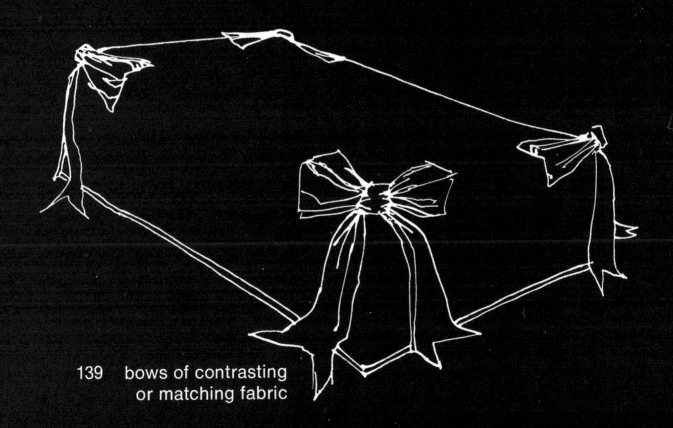

139 bows of contrasting
     or matching fabric

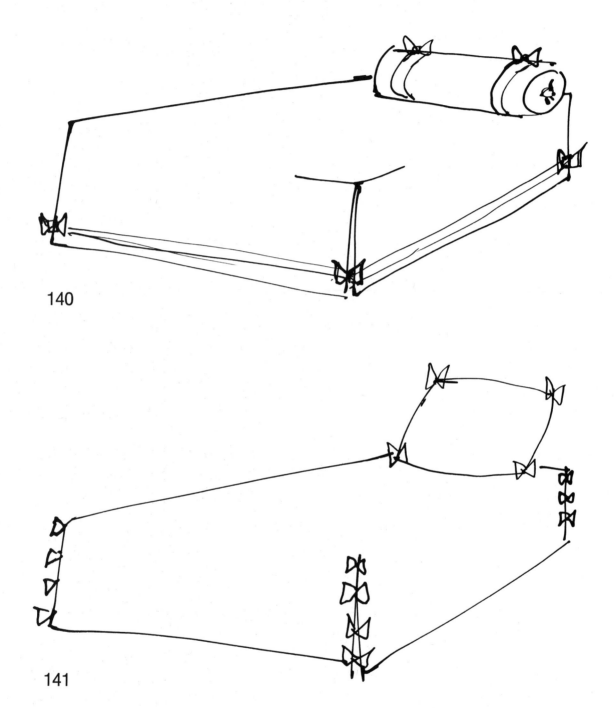

140

141

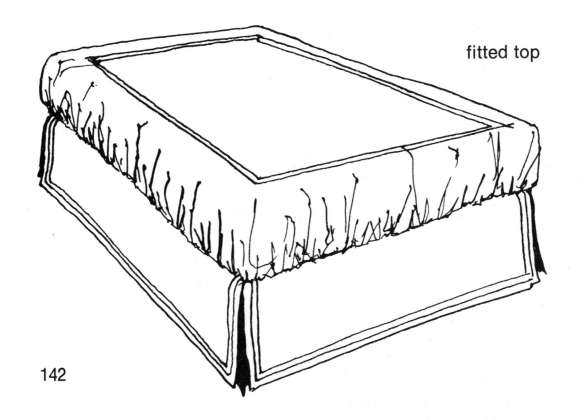

fitted top

142

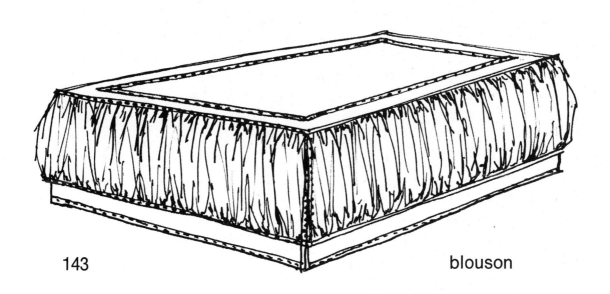

143

blouson

leather, fabric, or
felt cutout appliquéd

144

145   stuff poufy welt
with interlining

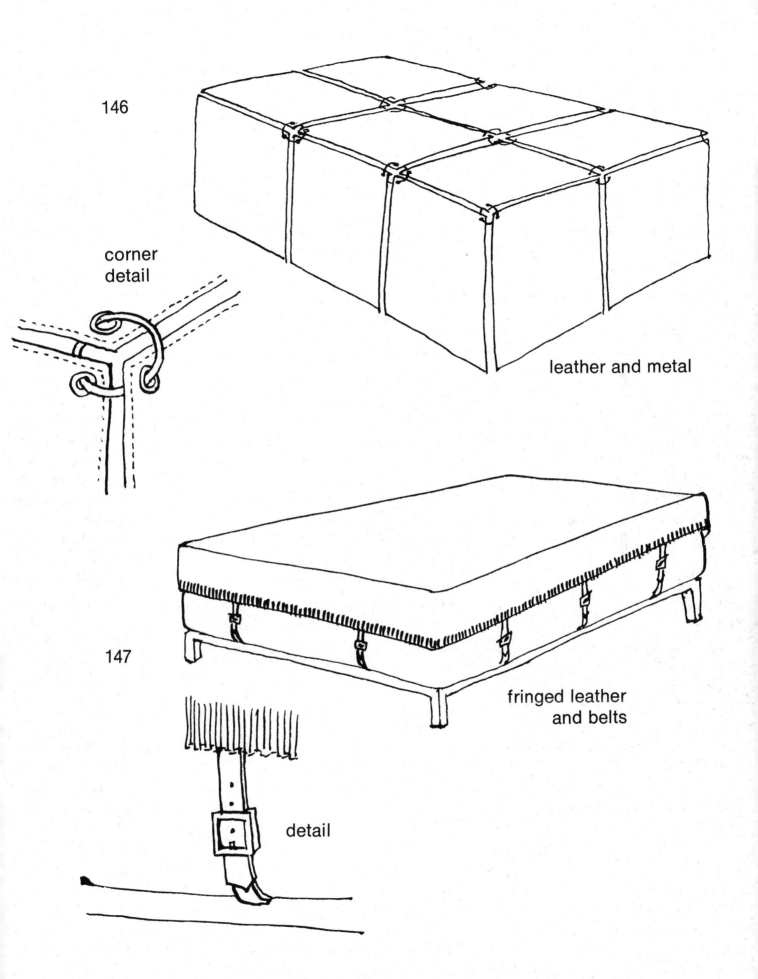

146

corner
detail

leather and metal

147

fringed leather
and belts

detail

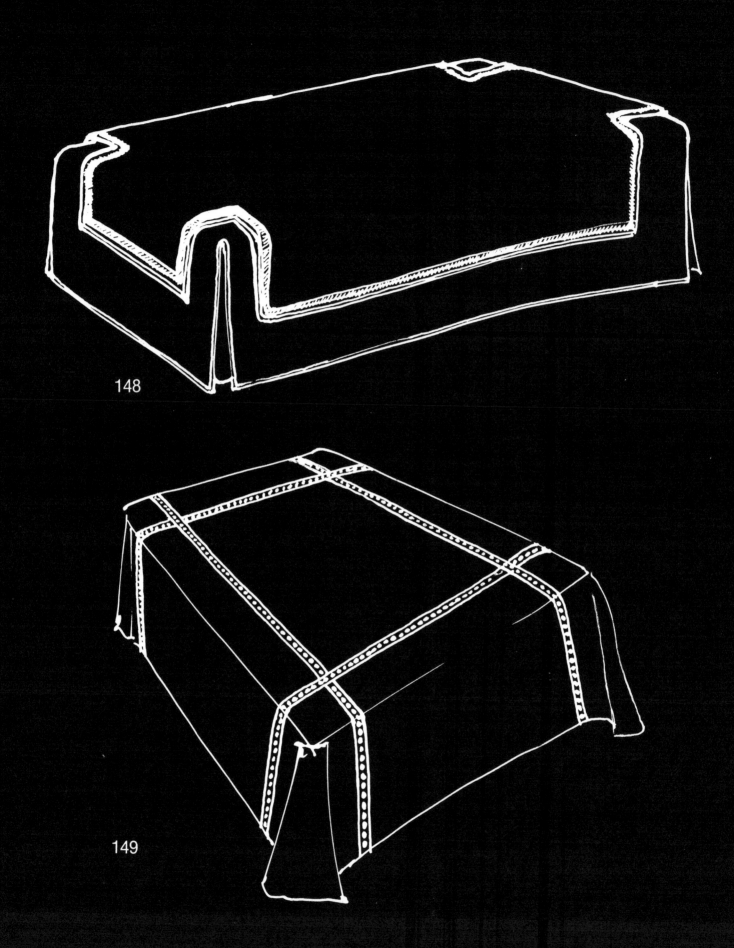

148

149

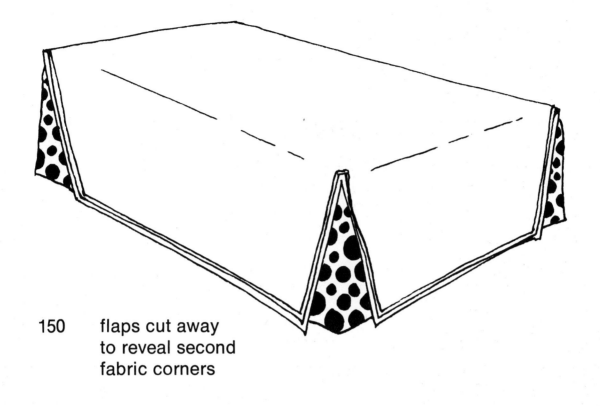

150   flaps cut away
       to reveal second
       fabric corners

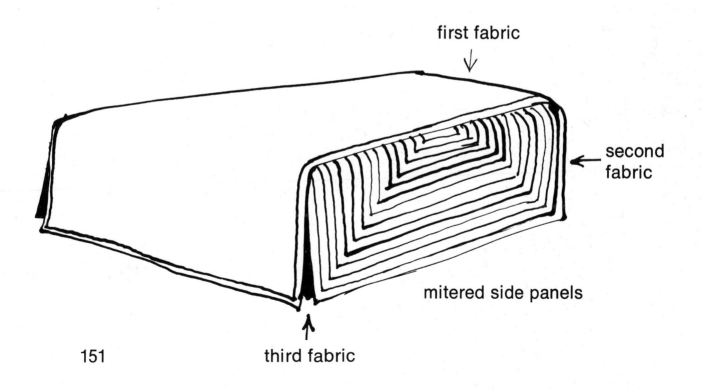

first fabric

second
fabric

mitered side panels

151   third fabric

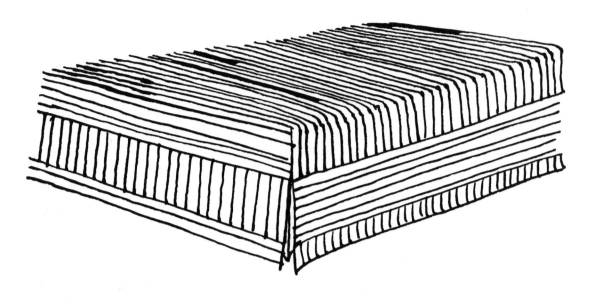

152   striped fabric pieced
together to form patterns

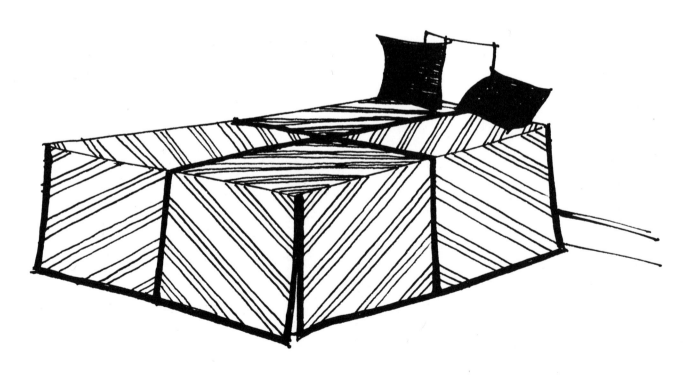

153   diagonally striped fabric
miter cut and outlined with tape

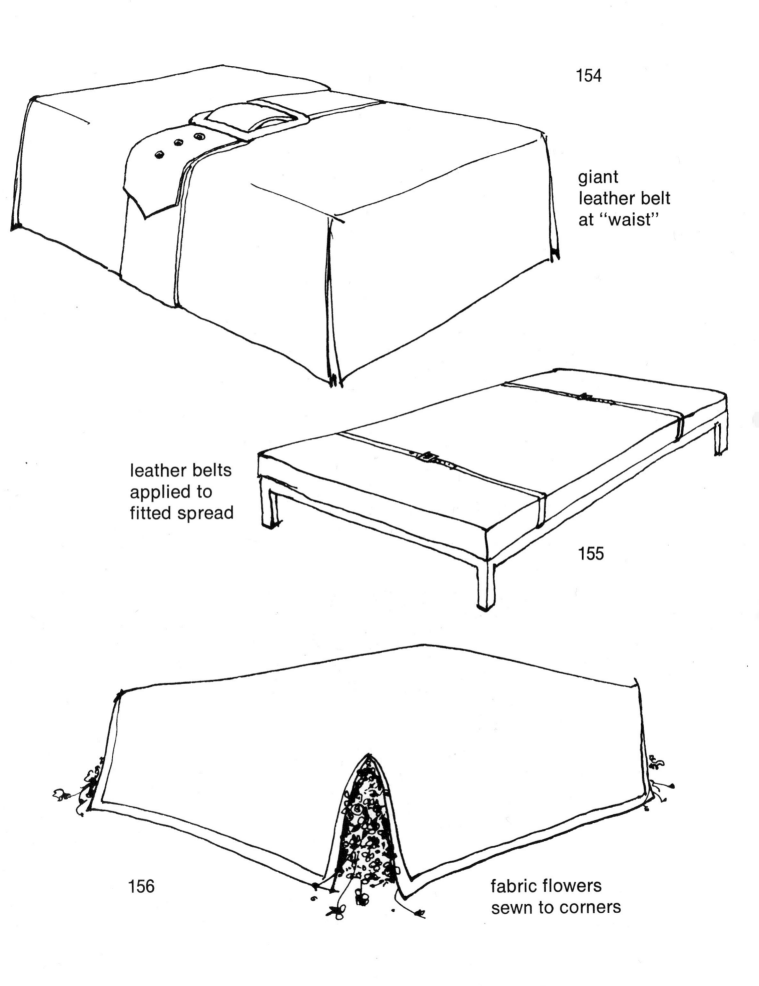

154

giant
leather belt
at "waist"

leather belts
applied to
fitted spread

155

156

fabric flowers
sewn to corners

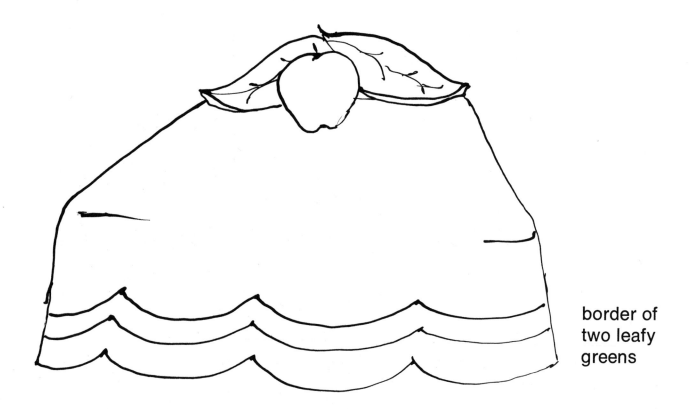

border of
two leafy
greens

157   leaf and fruit pillows on flower garden print

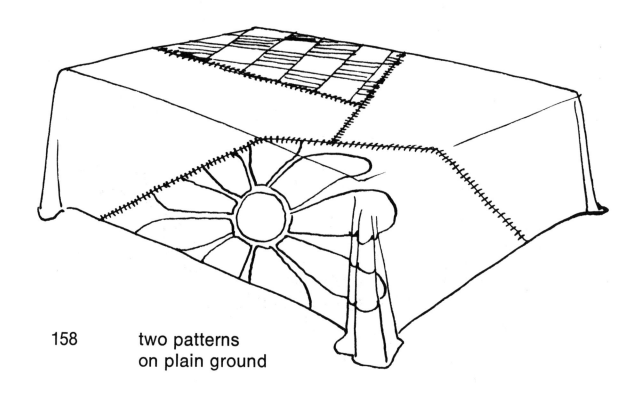

158   two patterns
on plain ground

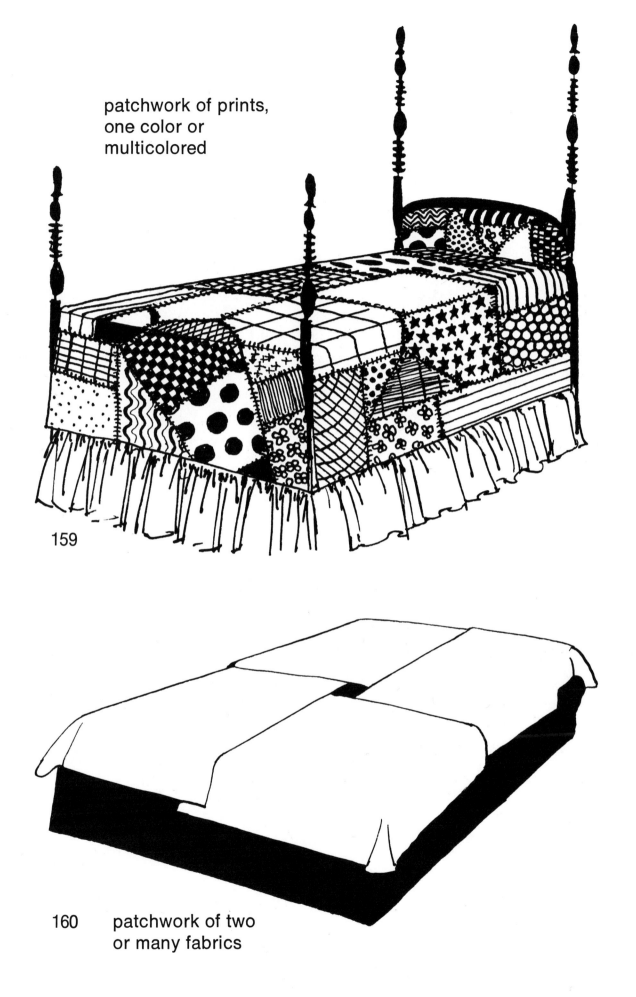

patchwork of prints,
one color or
multicolored

159

160   patchwork of two
       or many fabrics

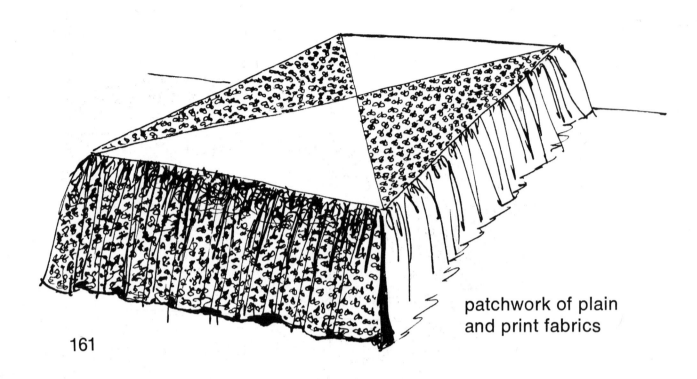

patchwork of plain
and print fabrics

161

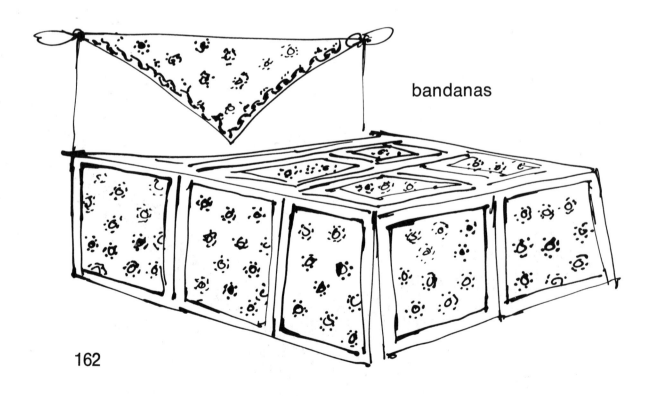

bandanas

162

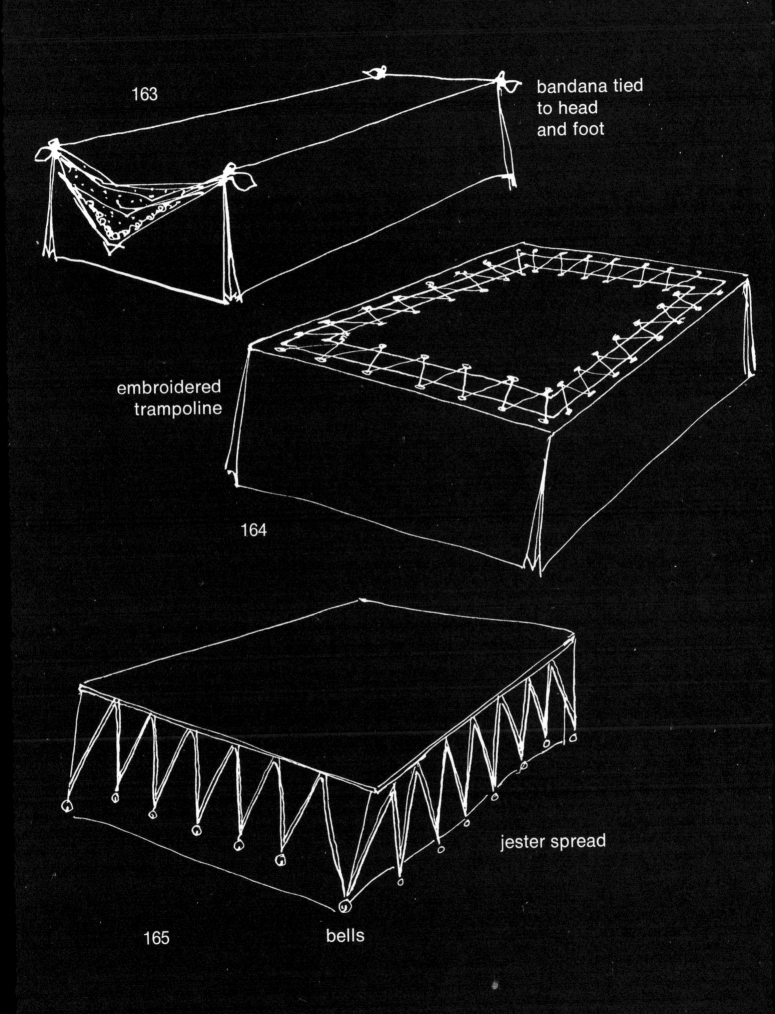

163   bandana tied to head and foot

embroidered trampoline

164

jester spread

165   bells

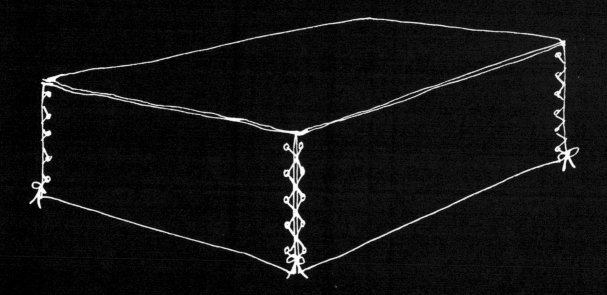

166   canvas, eyelets, rawhide

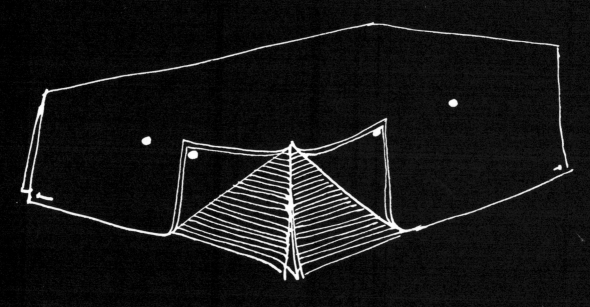

167   tent flap

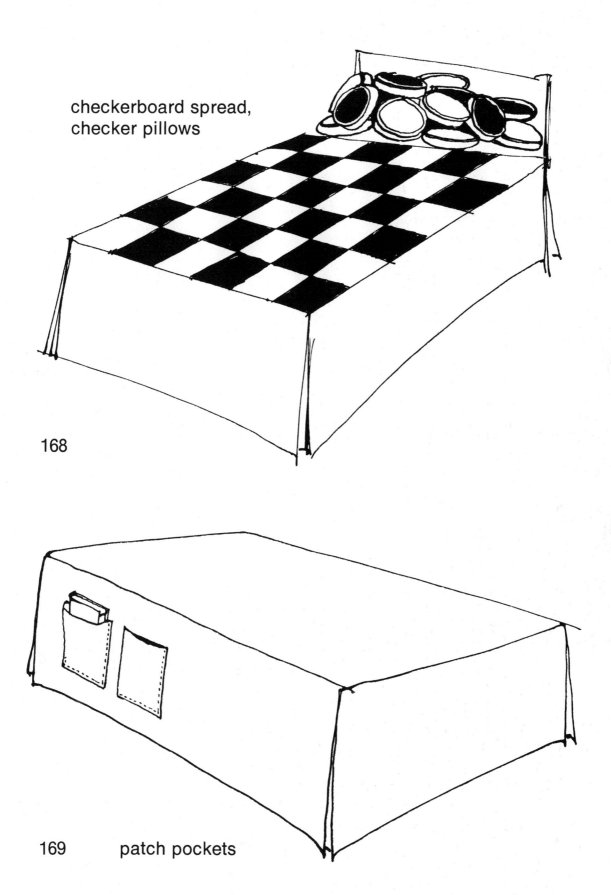

checkerboard spread,
checker pillows

168

169   patch pockets

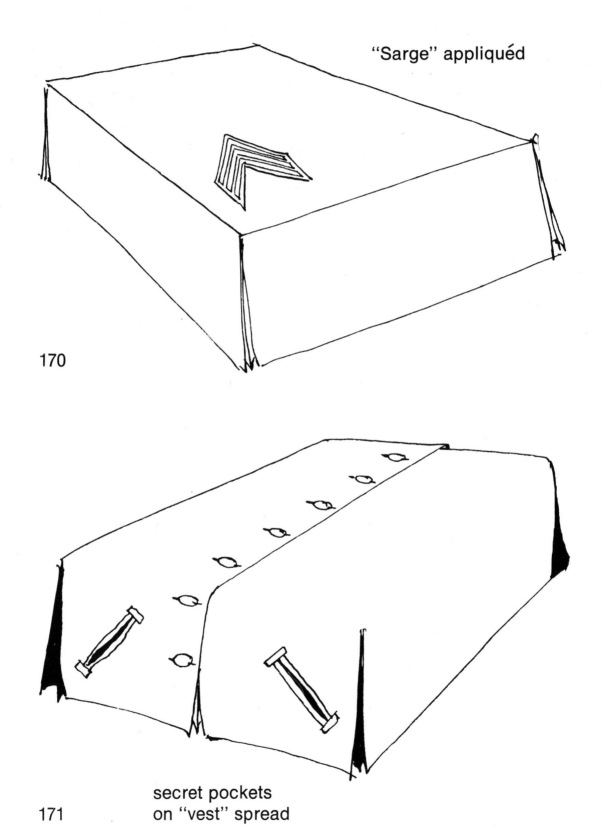

"Sarge" appliquéd

170

secret pockets
on "vest" spread

171

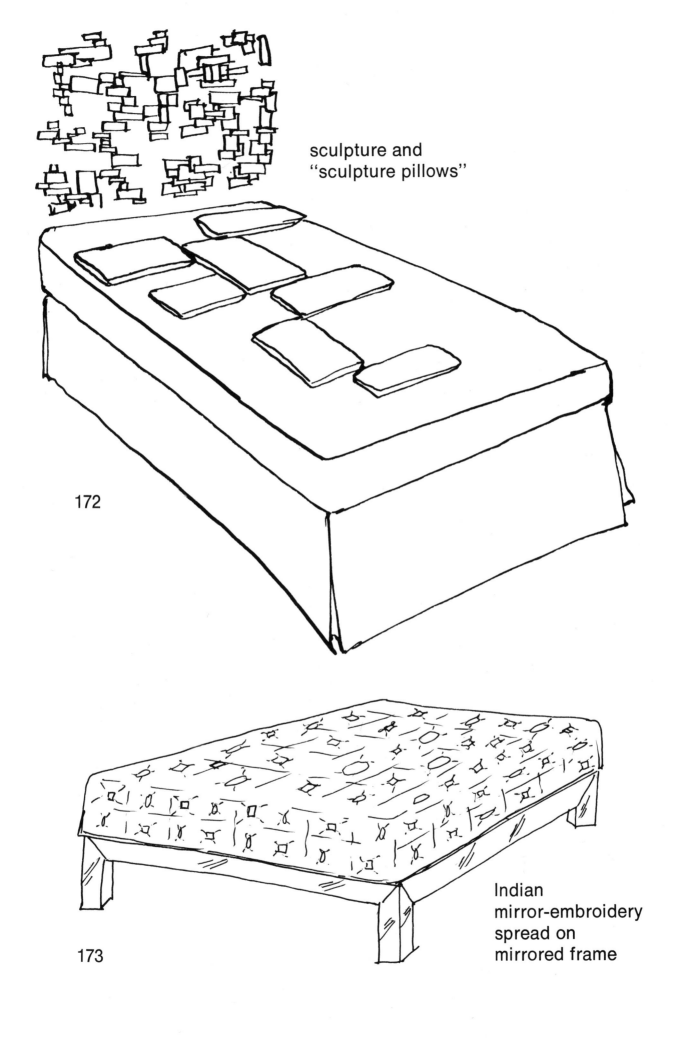

sculpture and "sculpture pillows"

172

173

Indian
mirror-embroidery
spread on
mirrored frame

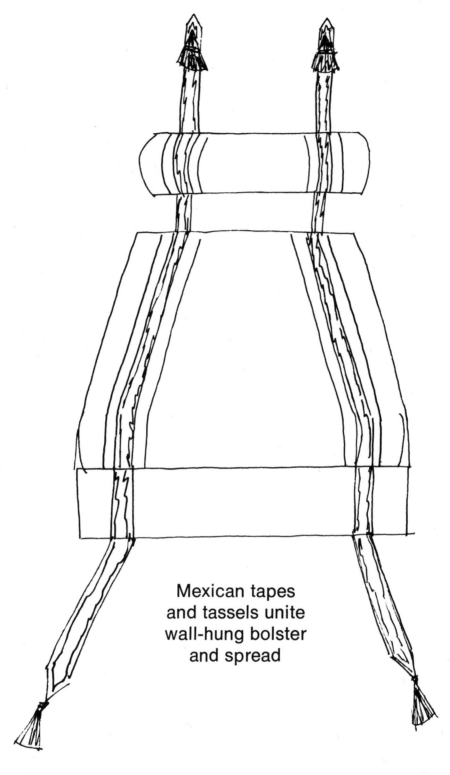

Mexican tapes
and tassels unite
wall-hung bolster
and spread

174

"sleeping bag" bolster
hung from hooks

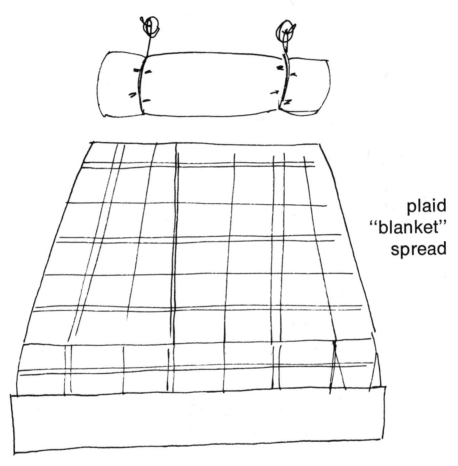

plaid
"blanket"
spread

frame or box spring
upholstered in tent canvas

175

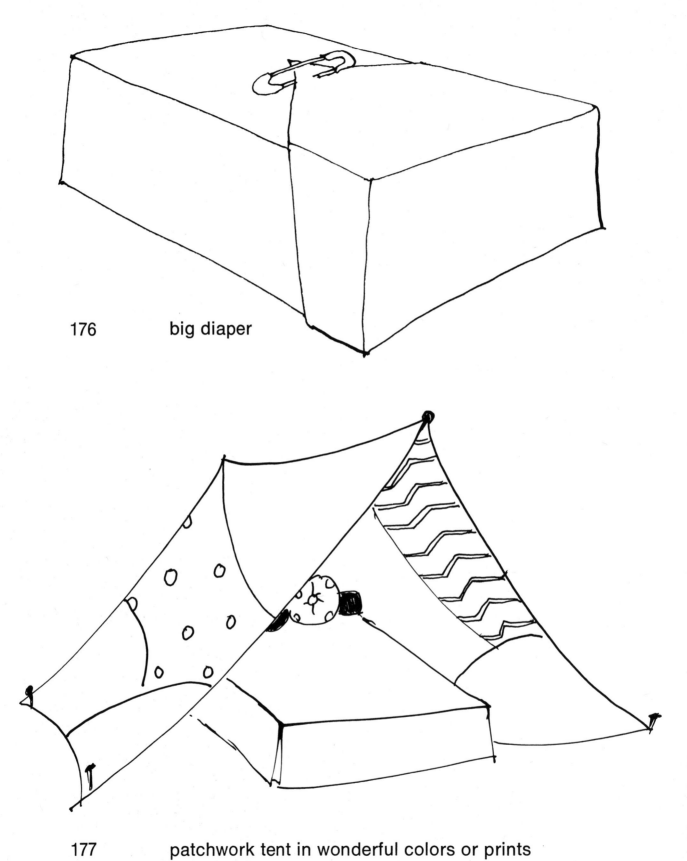

176   big diaper

177   patchwork tent in wonderful colors or prints

headboards
and
daybeds

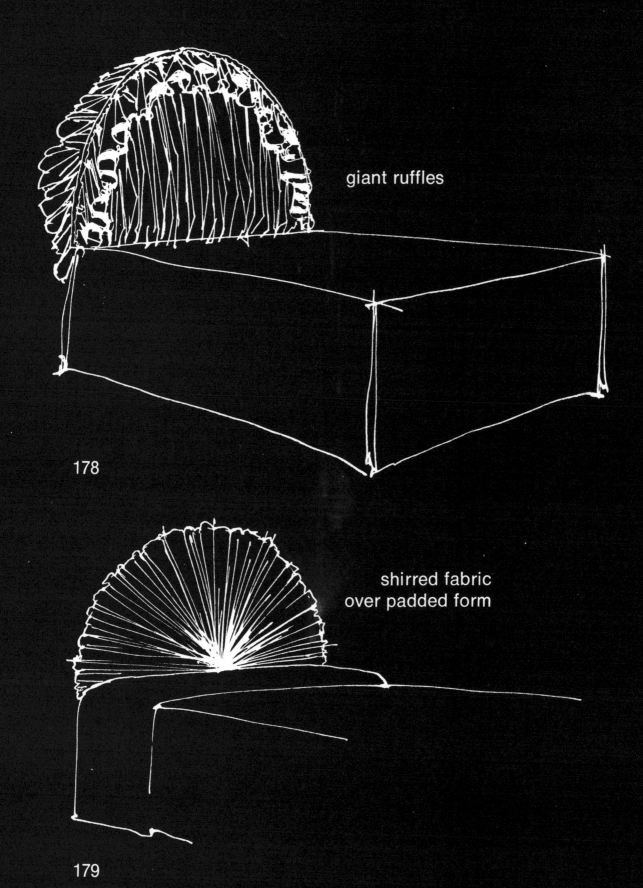

giant ruffles

178

shirred fabric
over padded form

179

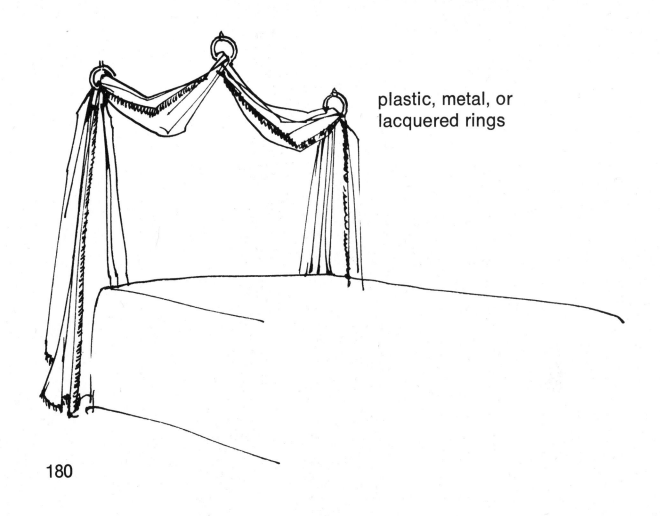

plastic, metal, or
lacquered rings

180

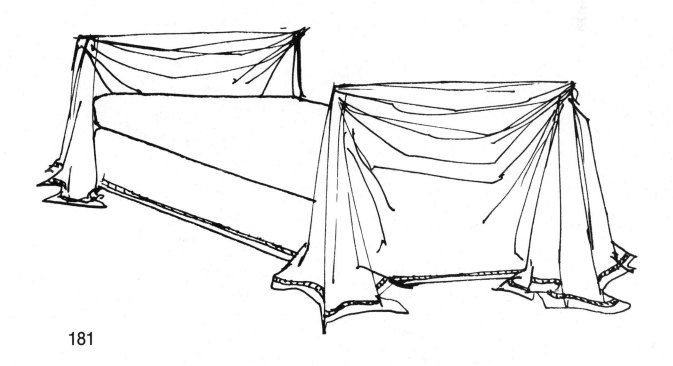

181

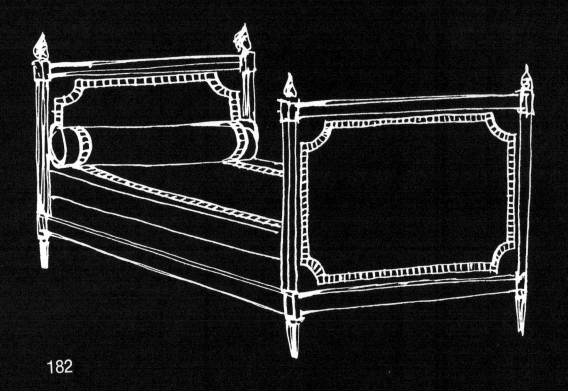

182

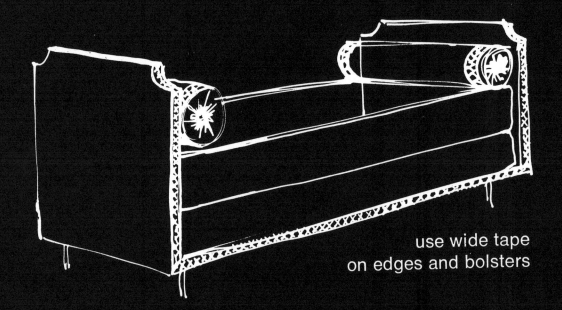

use wide tape
on edges and bolsters

183

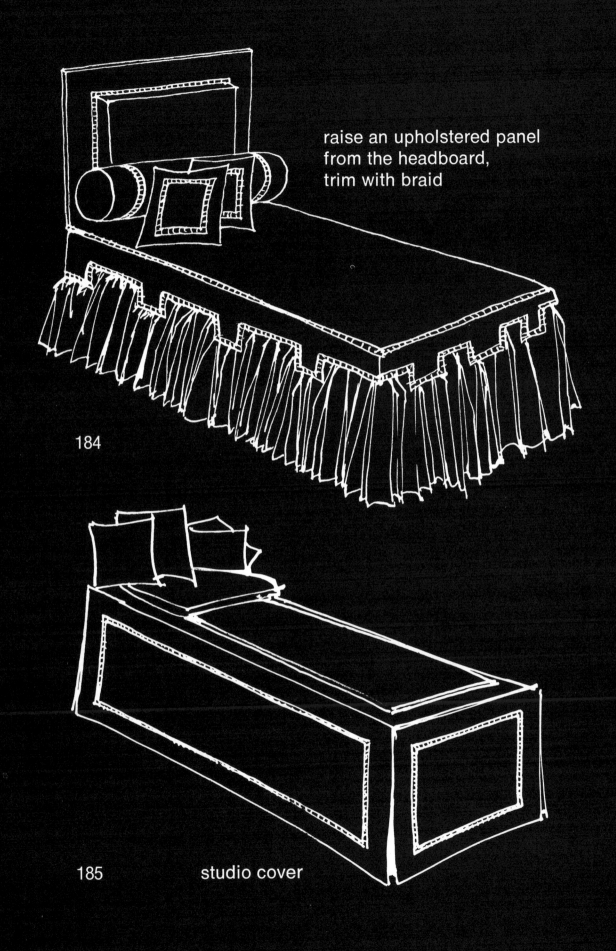

raise an upholstered panel
from the headboard,
trim with braid

184

185   studio cover

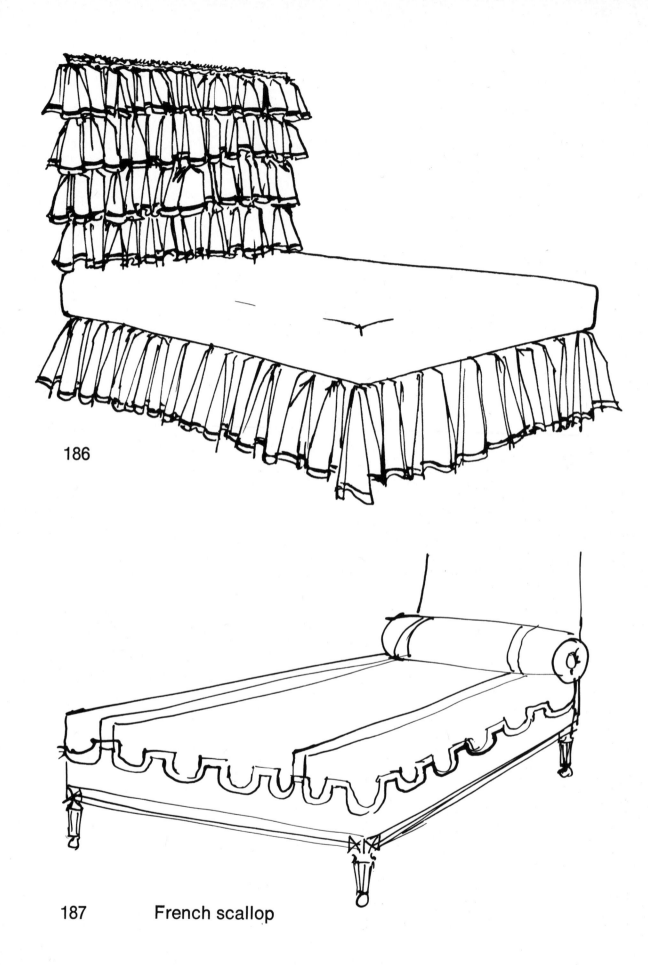

186

187   French scallop

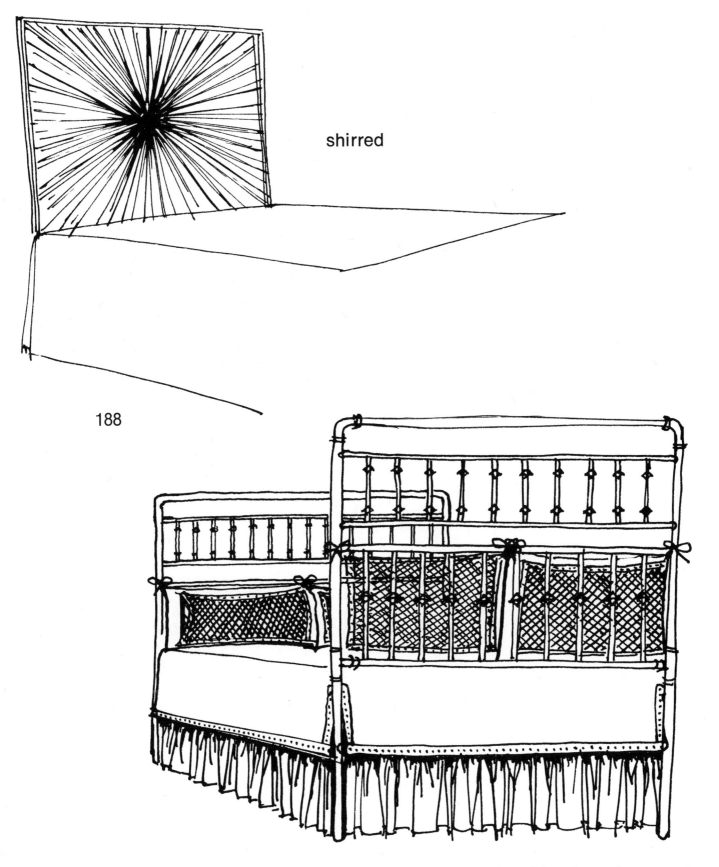

shirred

188

189   tie pillows to metal headboard and footboard

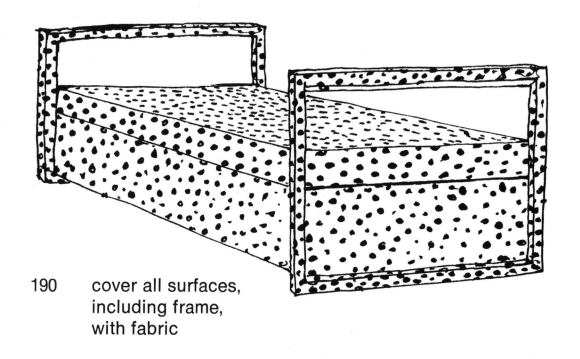

190   cover all surfaces,
       including frame,
       with fabric

leather "Chesterfield"
bed and spread

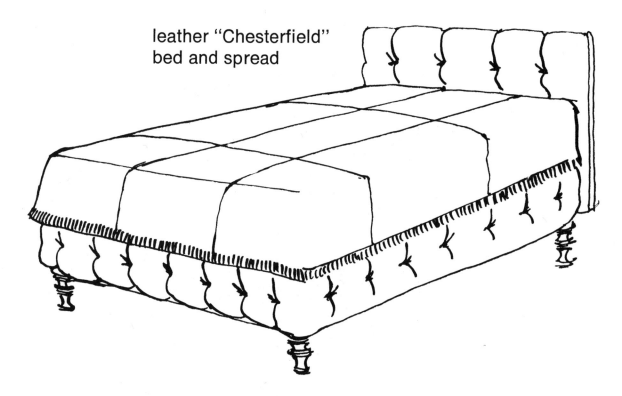

191

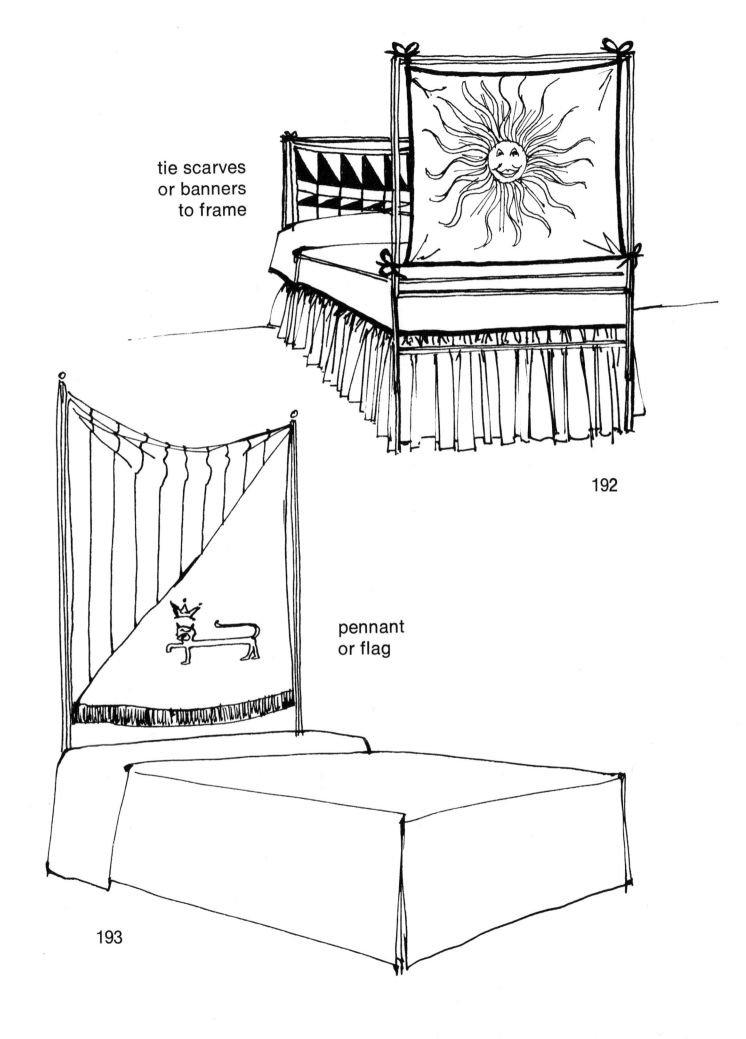

tie scarves
or banners
to frame

192

pennant
or flag

193

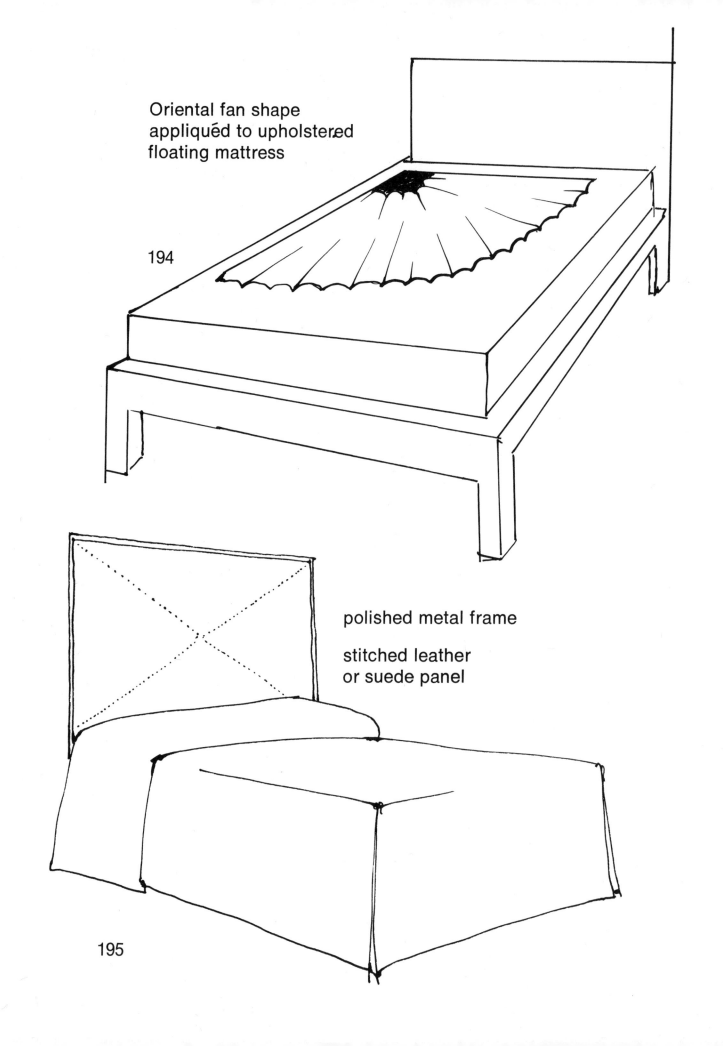

Oriental fan shape
appliquéd to upholstered
floating mattress

194

polished metal frame

stitched leather
or suede panel

195

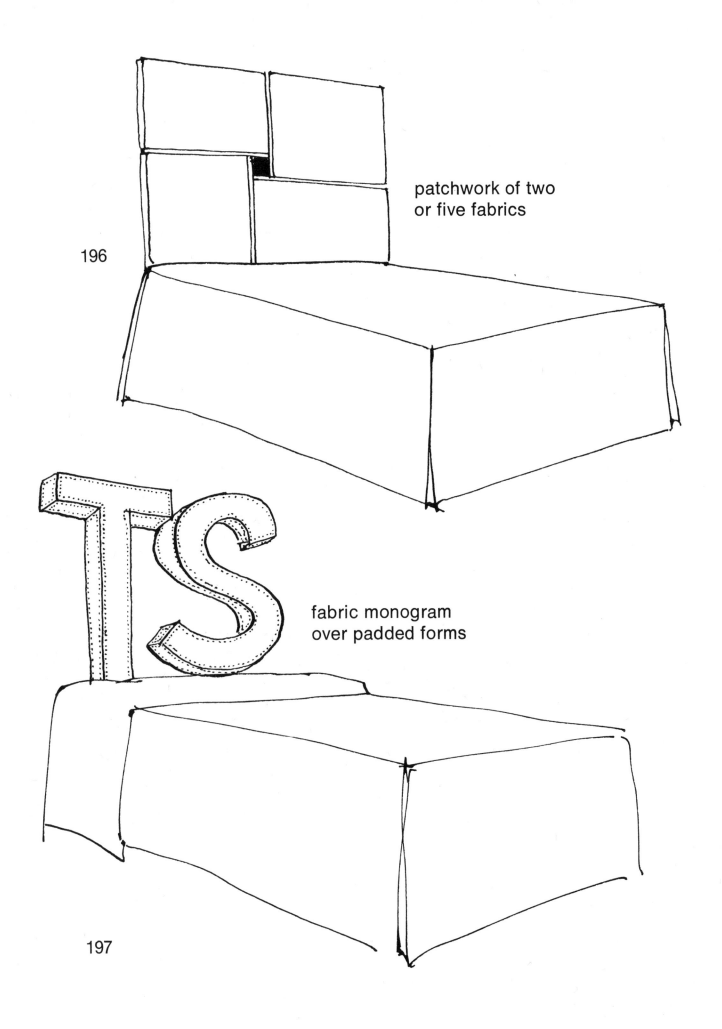

196

patchwork of two
or five fabrics

fabric monogram
over padded forms

197

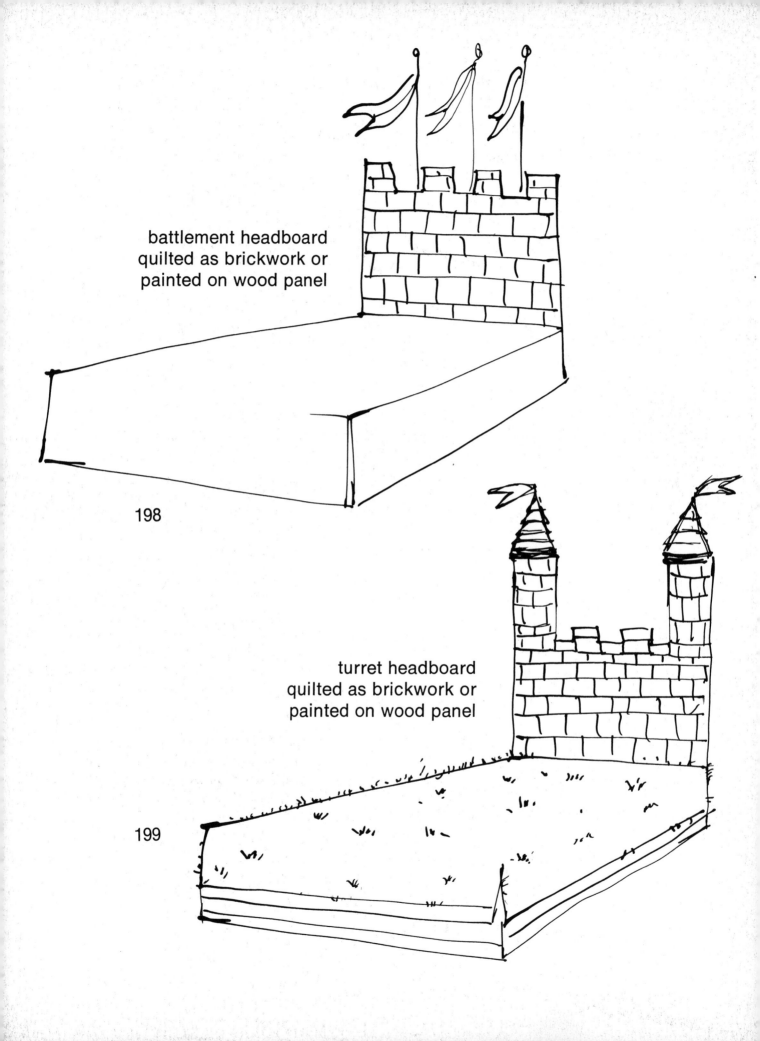

battlement headboard
quilted as brickwork or
painted on wood panel

198

turret headboard
quilted as brickwork or
painted on wood panel

199

patchwork clown cap

200

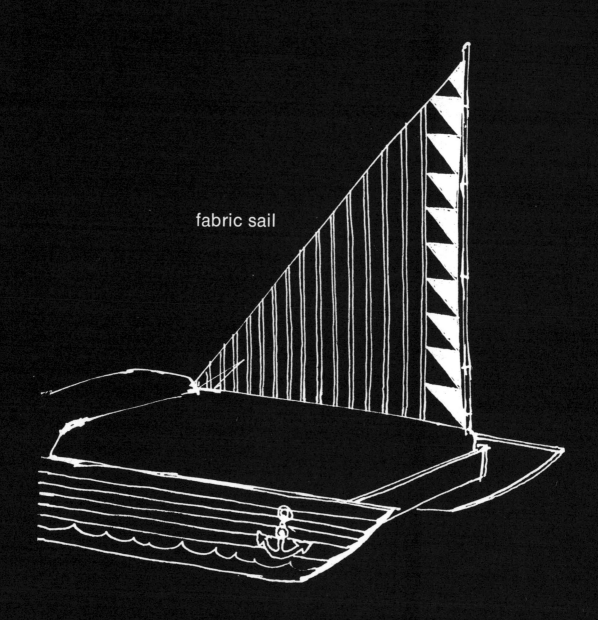

fabric sail

201

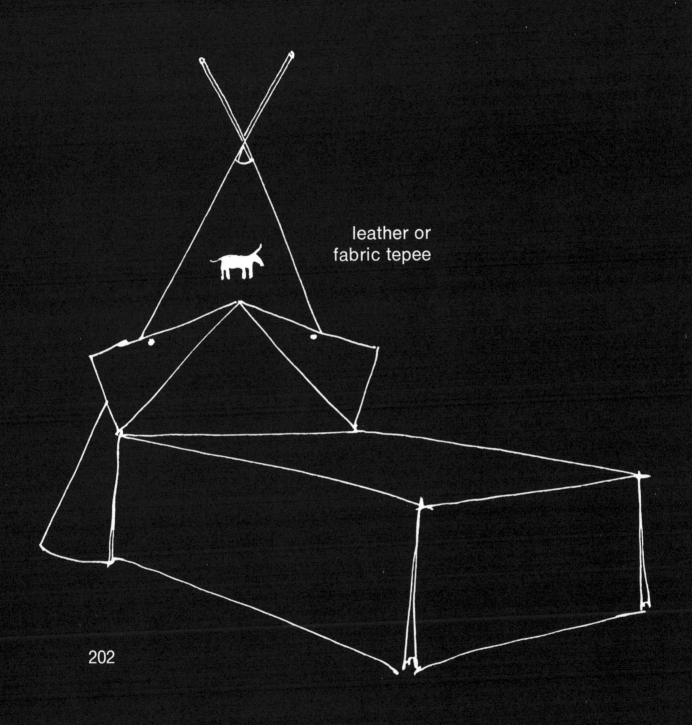

leather or
fabric tepee

202

203   large kite headboard,
       tail appliquéd on bedspread

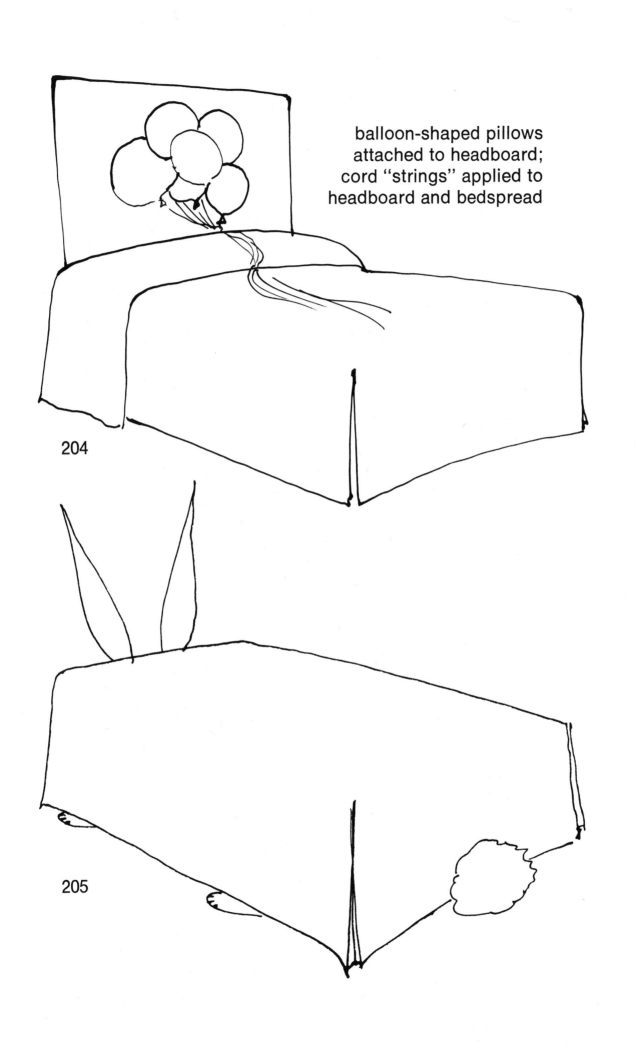

balloon-shaped pillows
attached to headboard;
cord "strings" applied to
headboard and bedspread

204

205

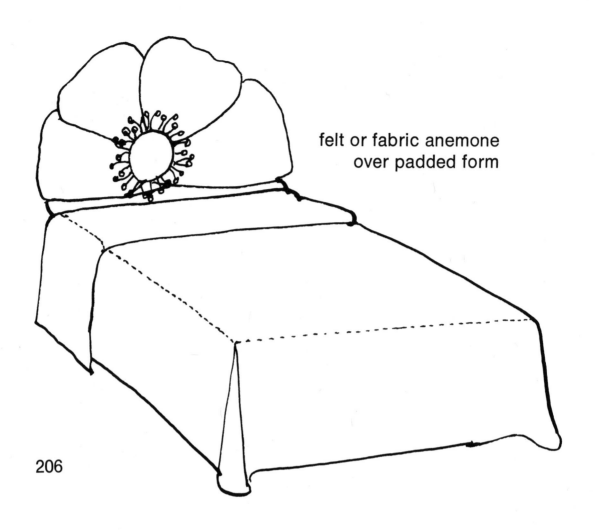

felt or fabric anemone
over padded form

206

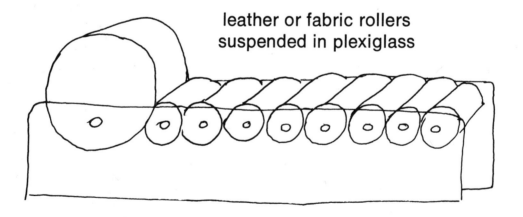

leather or fabric rollers
suspended in plexiglass

207

skirts

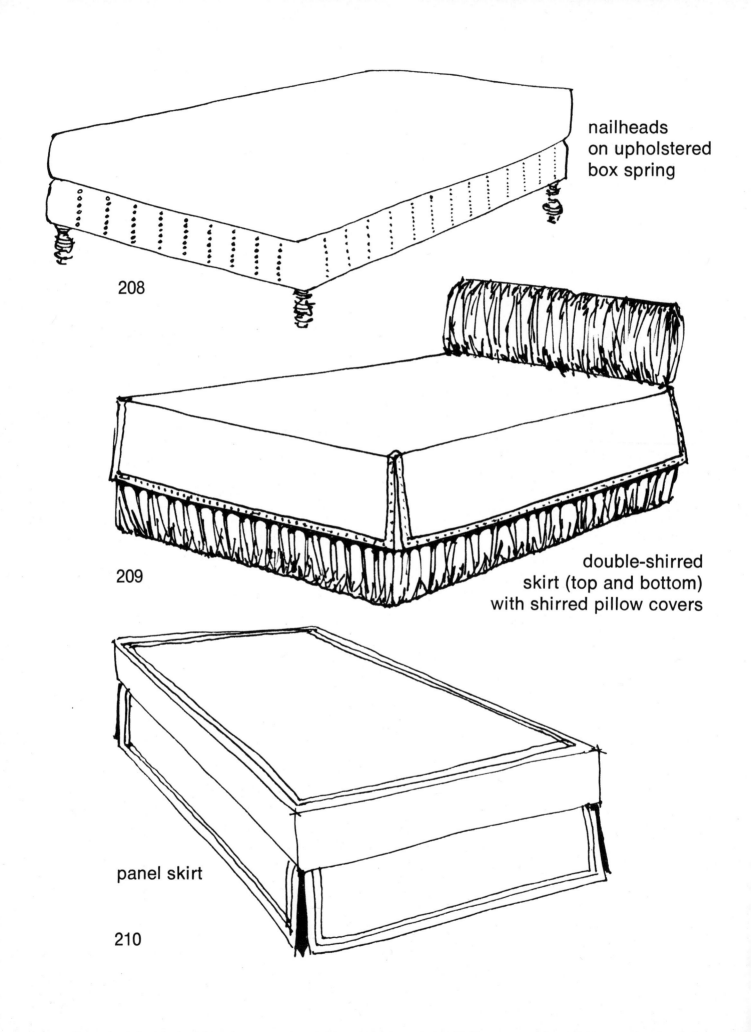

nailheads
on upholstered
box spring

208

double-shirred
skirt (top and bottom)
with shirred pillow covers

209

panel skirt

210

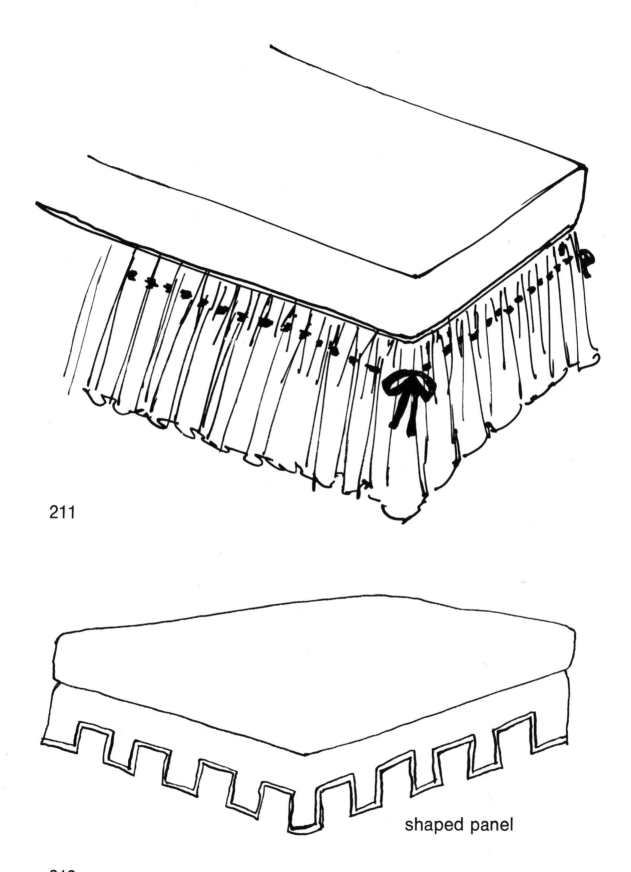

211

212

shaped panel

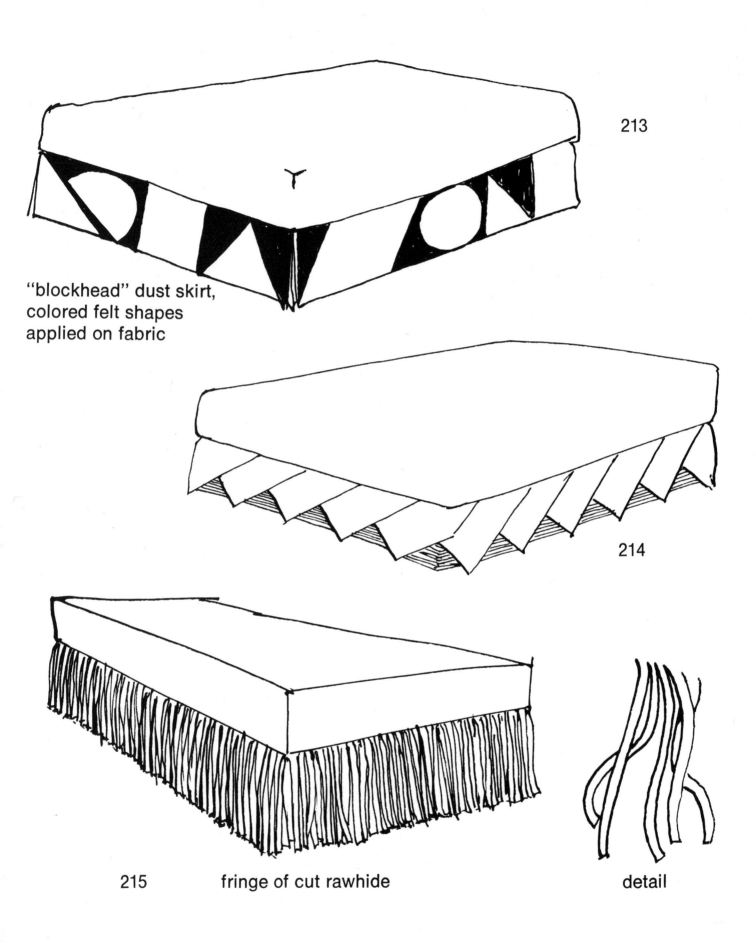

213

"blockhead" dust skirt,
colored felt shapes
applied on fabric

214

215   fringe of cut rawhide   detail

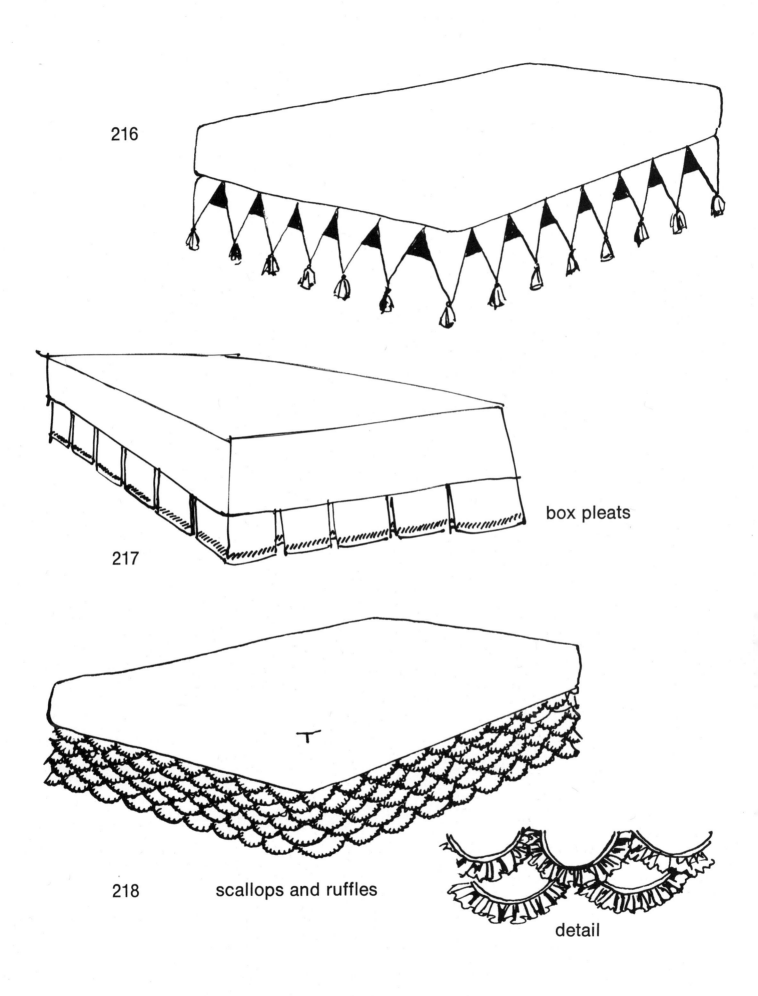

216

217 box pleats

218 scallops and ruffles detail

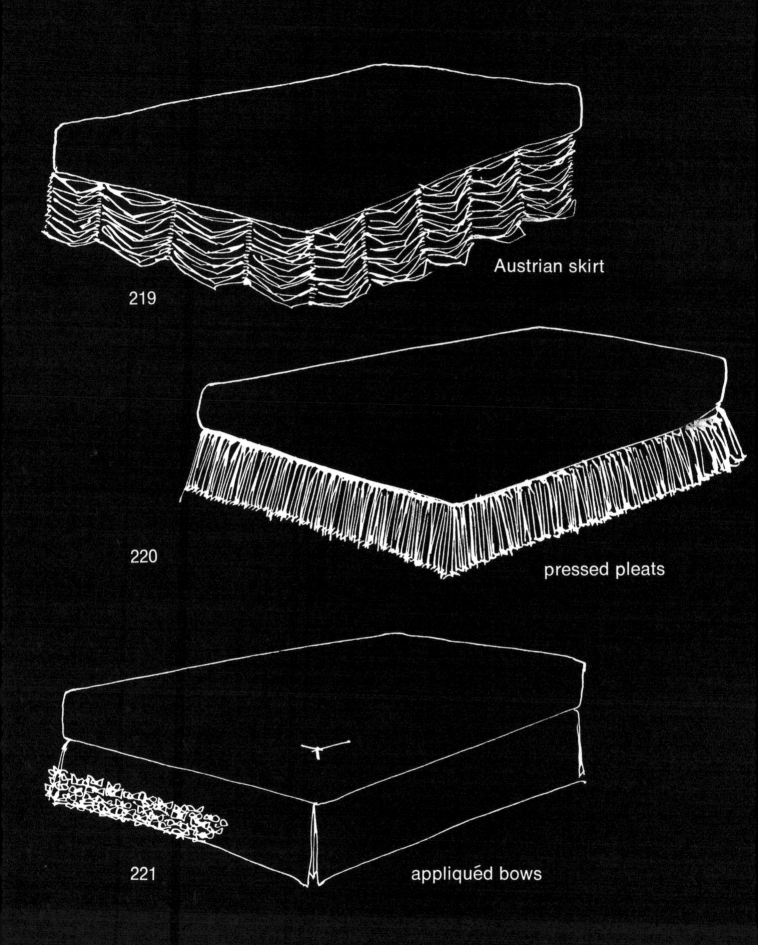

219   Austrian skirt

220   pressed pleats

221   appliquéd bows

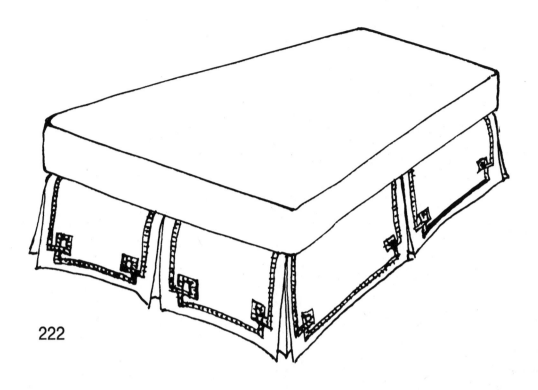

222

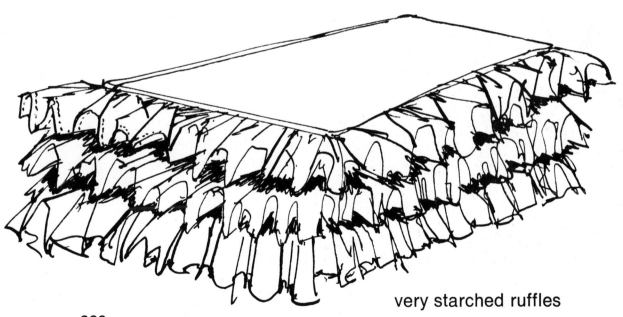

very starched ruffles

223

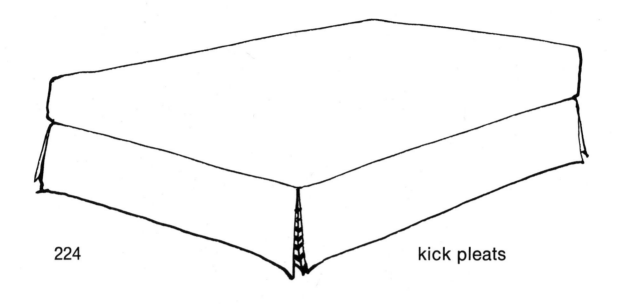

224   kick pleats

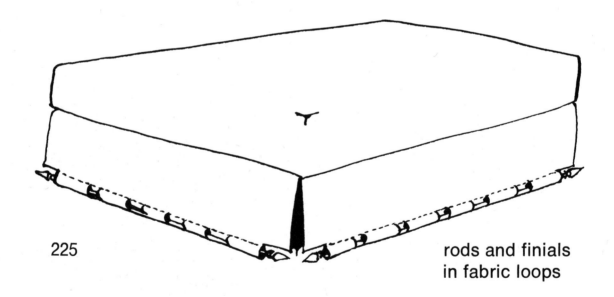

225   rods and finials
in fabric loops

quilting
and
appliqués

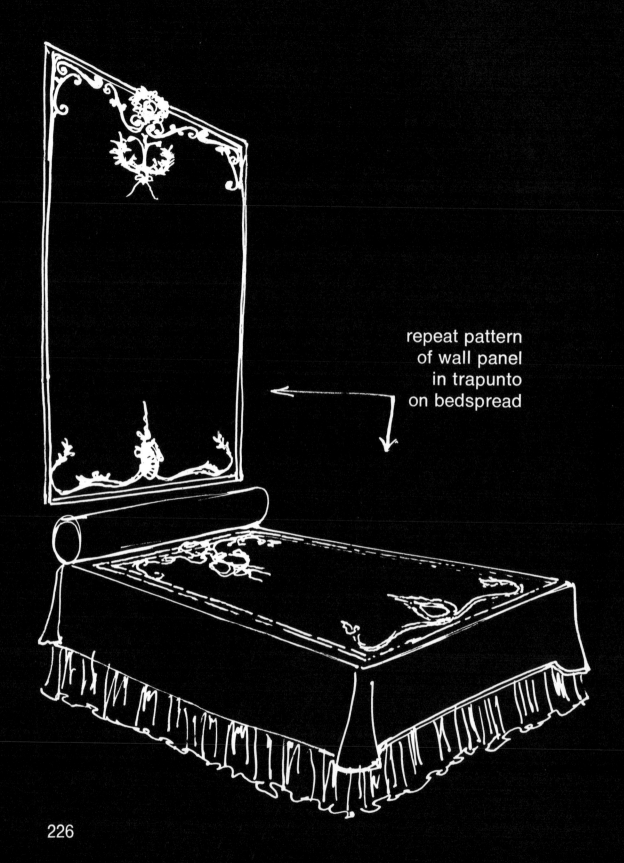

repeat pattern
of wall panel
in trapunto
on bedspread

226

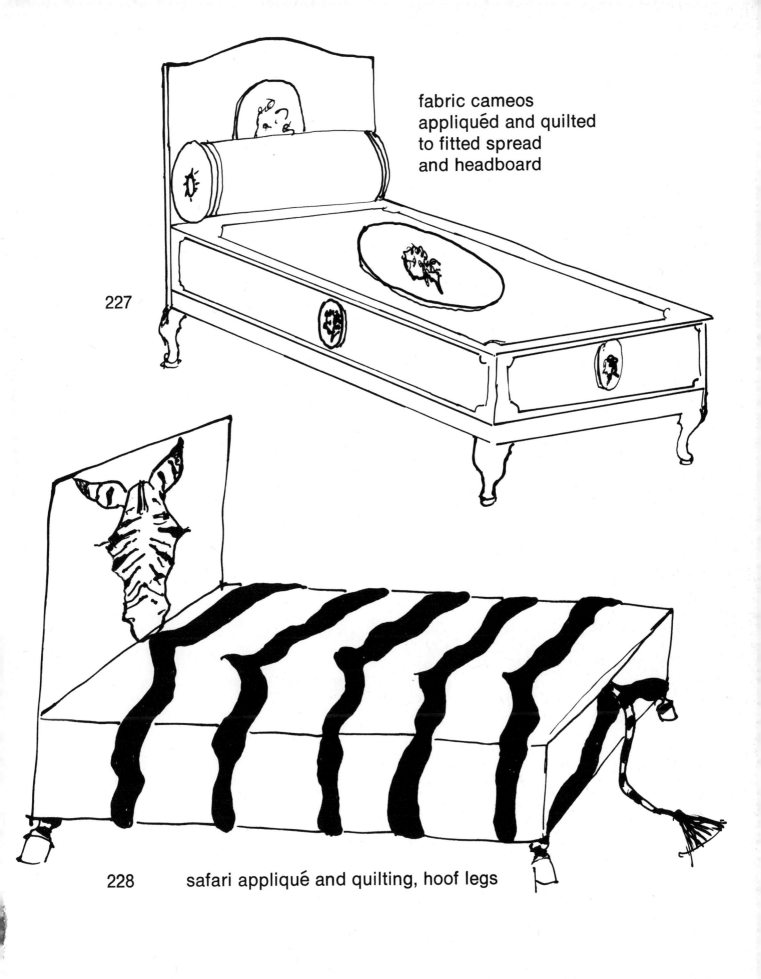

fabric cameos
appliquéd and quilted
to fitted spread
and headboard

227

228   safari appliqué and quilting, hoof legs

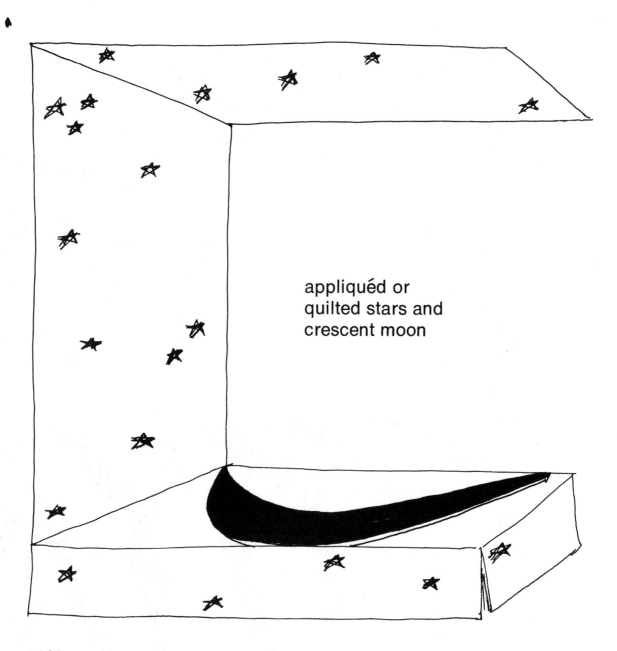

appliquéd or
quilted stars and
crescent moon

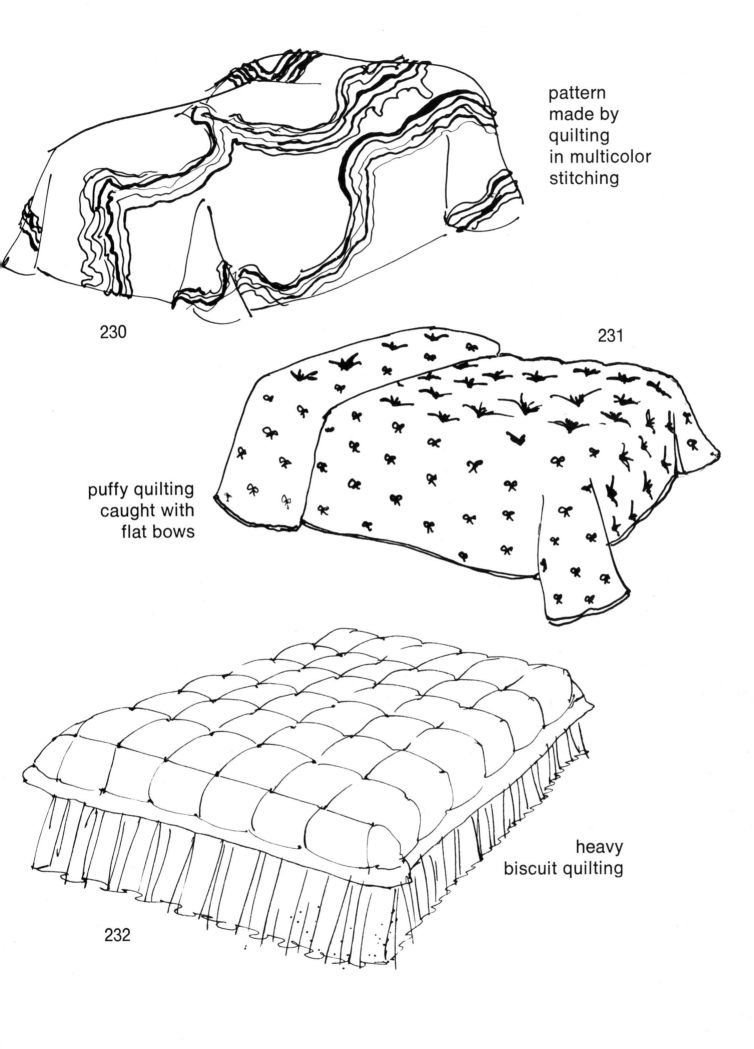

pattern
made by
quilting
in multicolor
stitching

230

231

puffy quilting
caught with
flat bows

heavy
biscuit quilting

232

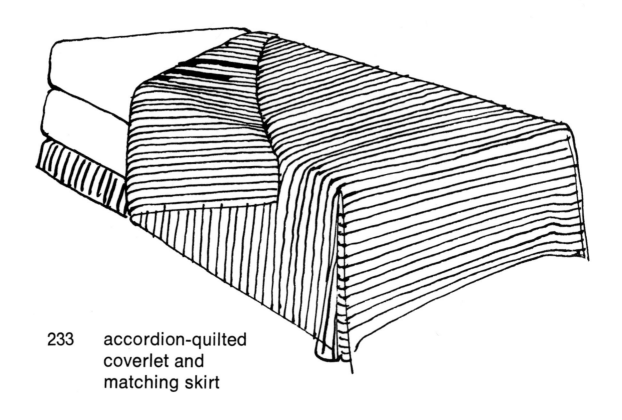

233 accordion-quilted
      coverlet and
      matching skirt

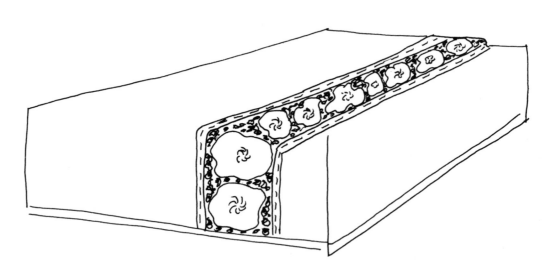

234 an obi asymmetrically
      placed on fitted spread

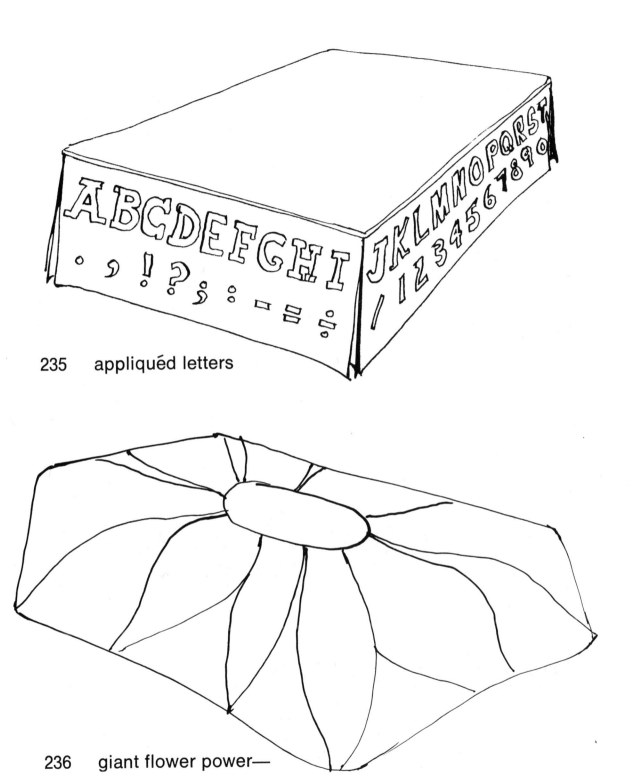

235   appliquéd letters

236   giant flower power—
       quilted and outline
       stitched in flower colors

237   appliquéd flower and pot

238   quilted monogram

index

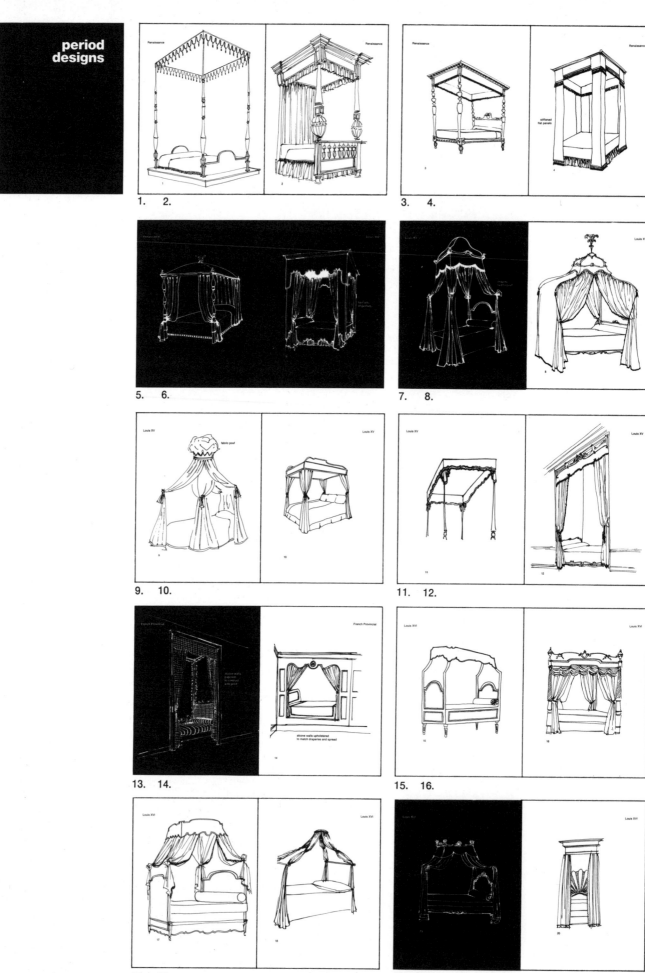

period designs

1. 2.

3. 4.

5. 6.

7. 8.

9. 10.

11. 12.

13. 14.

15. 16.

17. 18.

19. 20.

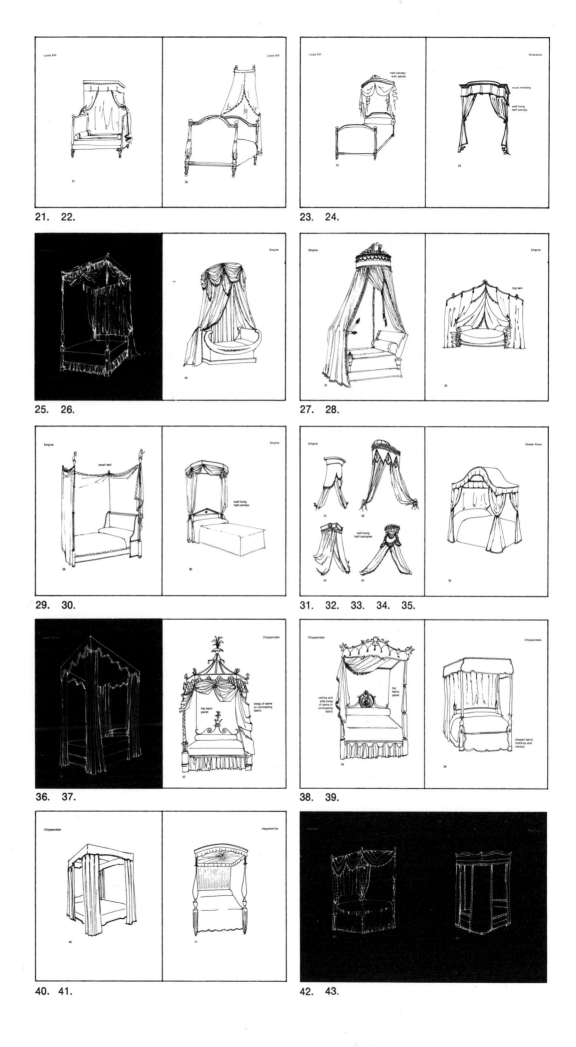

21. 22.

23. 24.

25. 26.

27. 28.

29. 30.

31. 32. 33. 34. 35.

36. 37.

38. 39.

40. 41.

42. 43.

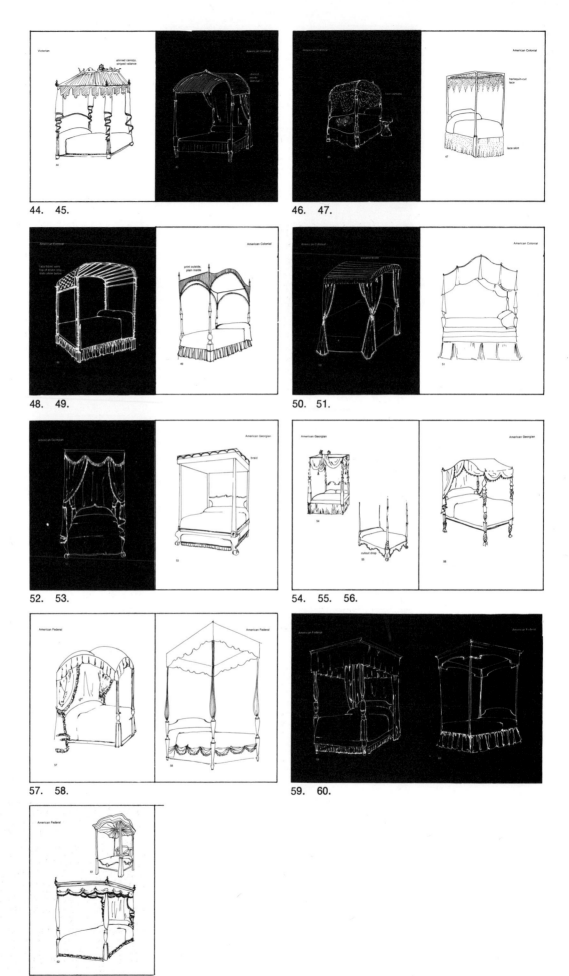

44. 45.

46. 47.

48. 49.

50. 51.

52. 53.

54. 55. 56.

57. 58.

59. 60.

61. 62.

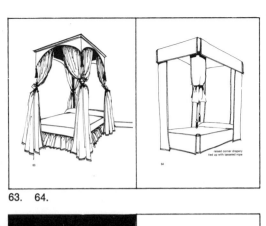

63. 64.

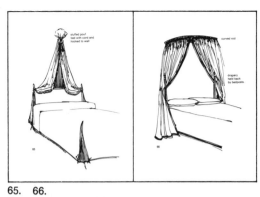

65. 66.

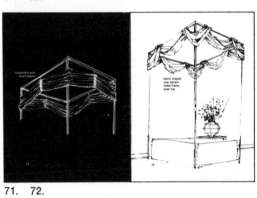

67. 68.

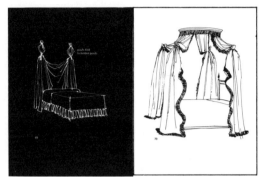

69. 70.

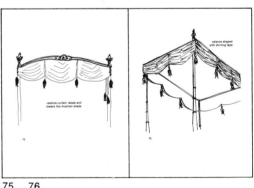

71. 72.

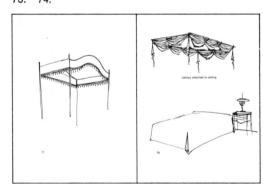

73. 74.

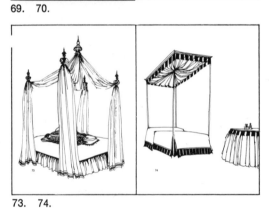

75. 76.

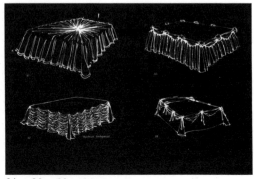

77. 78.

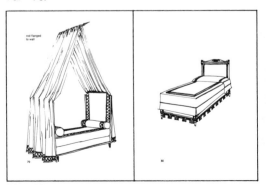

79. 80.

81. 82. 83. 84.

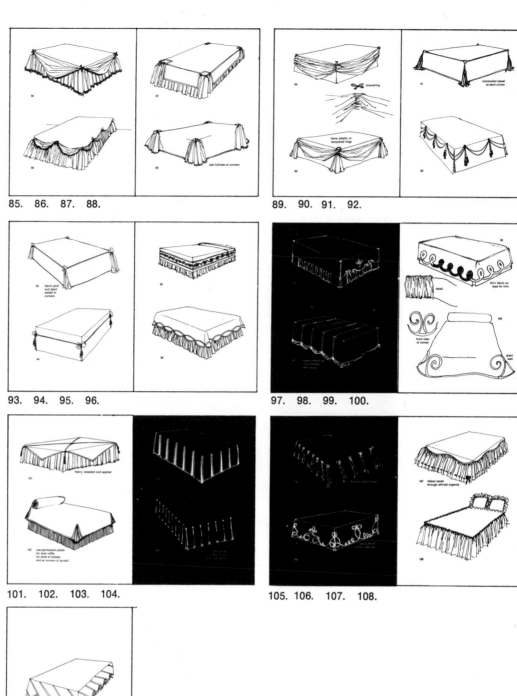

85.　86.　87.　88.

89.　90.　91.　92.

93.　94.　95.　96.

97.　98.　99.　100.

101.　102.　103.　104.

105.　106.　107.　108.

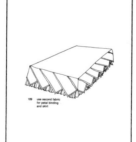

109.

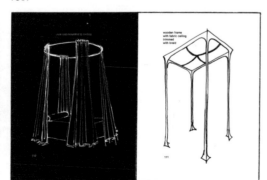

110.　111.

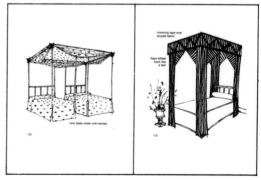

112.　113.

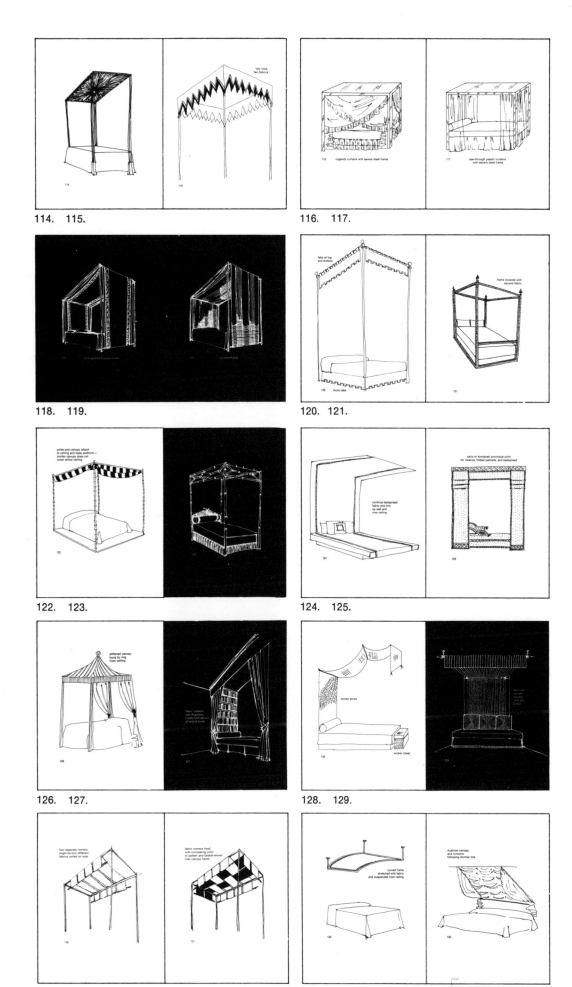

114. 115.

116. 117.

118. 119.

120. 121.

122. 123.

124. 125.

126. 127.

128. 129.

130. 131.

132. 133.

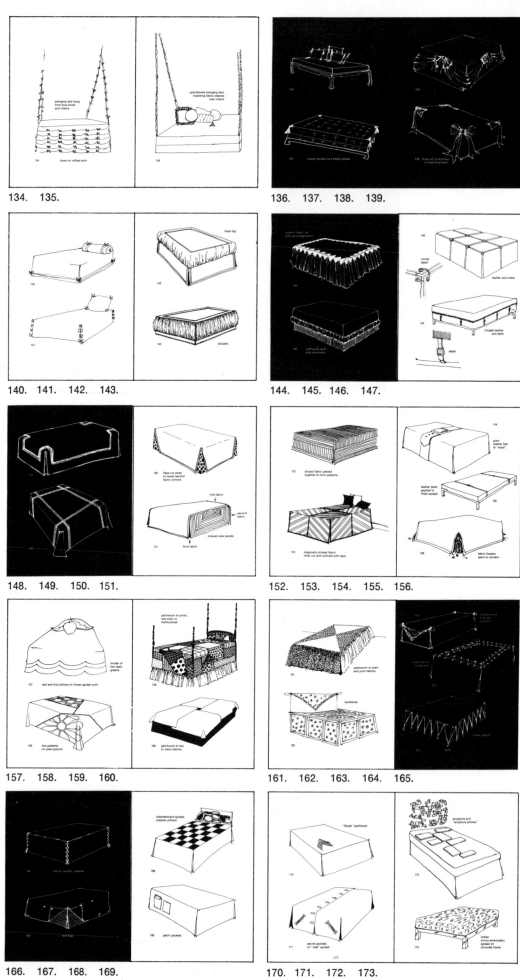

134. 135.

136. 137. 138. 139.

140. 141. 142. 143.

144. 145. 146. 147.

148. 149. 150. 151.

152. 153. 154. 155. 156.

157. 158. 159. 160.

161. 162. 163. 164. 165.

166. 167. 168. 169.

170. 171. 172. 173.

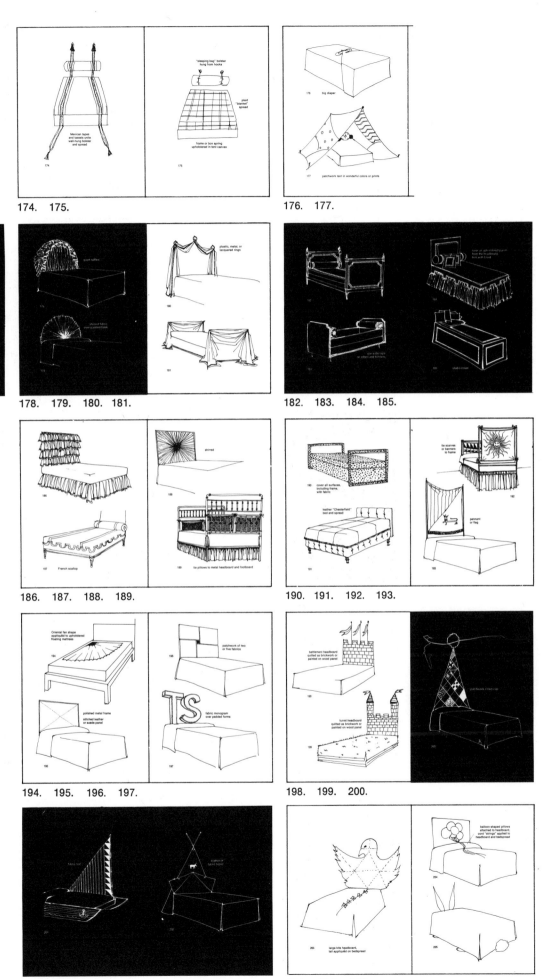

174. 175.

176. 177.

**headboards
and
daybeds**

178. 179. 180. 181.

182. 183. 184. 185.

186. 187. 188. 189.

190. 191. 192. 193.

194. 195. 196. 197.

198. 199. 200.

201. 202.

203. 204. 205.

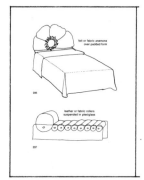

felt or fabric anemone
over padded form

leather or fabric rollers
suspended in plexiglass

206.　207.

skirts

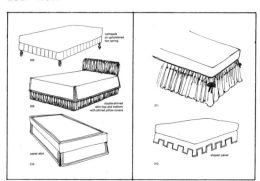

nailheads
on upholstered
box spring

double-shirred
skirt (top and bottom)
with shirred pillow covers

panel skirt

shaped panel

208.　209.　210.　211.　212.

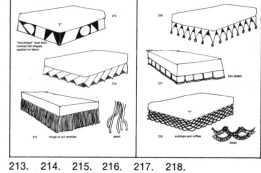

"blockhead" dust skirt,
colored felt shapes
applied on fabric

box pleats

fringe of cut rawhide

detail

scallops and ruffles

detail

213.　214.　215.　216.　217.　218.

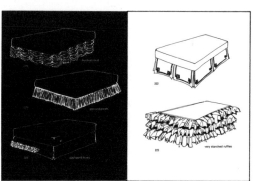

Austrian skirt

pennant pleats

appliquéd flowers

very starched ruffles

219.　220.　221.　222.　223.

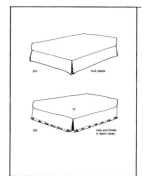

kick pleats

rods and finials
in fabric loops

224.　225.

**quilting
and
appliqués**

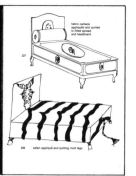

fabric cameos
appliquéd and quilted
to fitted spread
and headboard

repeat pattern
of wall panel
in trapunto
in bedspread

safari appliqué and quilting, hoof legs

226.　227.　228.

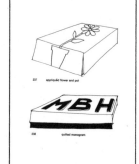

appliquéd or
quilted stars and
crescent moon

pattern
made by
quilting
in multicolor
stitching

puffy quilting
caught with
flat bows

heavy
biscuit quilting

229.　230.　231.　232.

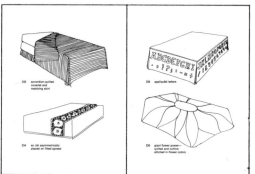

accordion-quilted
coverlet and
matching skirt

an obi asymmetrically
placed on fitted spread

appliquéd letters

giant flower power—
quilted and outline
stitched in flower colors

appliquéd flower and pot

quilted monogram

233.　234.　235.　236.

237.　238.